*How
Equal Temperament
Ruined Harmony*

How
Equal Temperament
Ruined Harmony

(and Why You Should Care)

Ross W. Duffin

W. W. Norton & Company
New York · London

For information about permission to reproduce selections from this book, write to Permissions, W. W. Norton & Company, Inc., 500 Fifth Avenue, New York, NY 10110

Manufacturing by RR Donnelley, Bloomsburg
Book design by Charlotte Staub
Production manager: Anna Oler

Library of Congress Cataloging-in-Publication Data

Duffin, Ross W.
How equal temperament ruined harmony (and why you should care) /
Ross W. Duffin.—1st ed.
p. cm.
Includes bibliographical references and index.
ISBN 978-0-393-06227-4 (hardcover)
1. Musical temperament. I. Title.
ML3809.D84 2007
784.192'8—dc22   2006020903

ISBN 978-0-393-33420-3 pbk.

W. W. Norton & Company, Inc.
500 Fifth Avenue, New York, N.Y. 10110
www.wwnorton.com

W. W. Norton & Company Ltd.
15 Carlisle Street, London W1D 3BS

For my son,
David Simmons-Duffin

Contents

Acknowledgments

After I had made a first draft of this book, I actively sought the reaction of many musicians from a variety of backgrounds. Some are specialists on various tuning systems; others knew only equal temperament. Some are experienced in historical performance; others have made their careers as "modern" musicians. All are wonderful and thoughtful performers or music lovers whom I know and am fortunate enough to be able to importune in this way. Their criticisms, arguments, comments, questions, corrections, musings, and additional examples have contributed enormously to the book in its final form.

Among keyboard specialists, first of all, I must thank Bradley Lehman, Christopher Stembridge, Byron Schenkman, Willard Martin, Steven Lubin, Dana Gooley, David Breitman, and Peter Bennett. Wind players who read and commented include Debra Nagy, Bruce Haynes, and Ardal Powell. String players include David Douglass, Robert Mealy, Mary Springfels, Christina Babich, David Miller, Fred Fehleisen, Alan Harrell, Merry Peckham, and Peter Salaff. Physicists, critics, family members, and others with valuable insights include Herbert W. Myers, Cyrus Taylor, Donald Rosenberg, Paul Rapoport, Selena Simmons-Duffin, Jacalyn Duffin, and David Wolfe. I am grateful to them all for their constructive criticisms but, most of all, for their enthusiasm for the book and its message.

My wife, Beverly Simmons, too, contributed her usual expert mix of copyediting and cheerleading and, once again, tolerated my frequent distraction as I immersed myself in the book. She also provided indispensable assistance in obtaining many of the images that help make the book so vivid.

Thanks are due also to Philip Neuman for his inimitable cartoons. I had Phil's vision of the musical world in mind from the start, and I hope his contributions will help make the book's contents even more memorable.

I am grateful also to several people who assisted in various ways in procuring information or materials for the book: Joanna Ball, Carol Lynn Ward Bamford, Jeremy Barande, Manuel Op de Coul, E. Michael and Patricia Frederick, Cara Gilgenbach, Rebecca Harris-Warrick, Carl Mariani, Sally Pagan, Jeffrey Quick, Roger Savage, Kenneth Slowik, Gary Sturm, Stephen Toombs, Daniel Zager, and Michael Zarky.

I would also like to acknowledge a debt to *The New Grove Dictionary of Music and Musicians*. While this book is about tuning, the biographical sketches contained herein are intended as background, to help set that central discussion into some kind of personal and historical context. No one can do work in musical biography these days without consulting *The New Grove* and, indeed, many of my sketches are indebted to its articles. The reader is referred to them for further information.

I am grateful to W. W. Norton & Company for getting excited about a project that must have seemed completely "off the wall" when it first arrived. In particular, I would like to thank my editor, Maribeth Anderson Payne, her assistants Courtney Fitch and Graham Norwood, along with Nancy Palmquist, Don Rifkin, Neil Hoos, Anna Oler, Sue Llewellyn, and a host of other professionals who helped make this book what it is.

Finally, the one person I have omitted from the list of readers above was, in fact, the first person to read a draft "hot off the press" from my computer: my son, David Simmons-Duffin. He is also the only person to have afterward requested a later version so he could see what changes I had made. As an adolescent, devoted music listener, and novice violinist, David was already noticing and asking about temperaments, and reading Easley Blackwood's daunting *Structure of Recognizable Diatonic Tunings* with pleasure and profit. A few years later, as a physicist, avid amateur musician, and earliest reader of this book, he had many comments that were exceptionally helpful in clarifying my presentation of the material to a nonspecialist audience, in refining the technical language (though any shortcomings that remain are my own responsibility), and in improving the logic of my argument. One of his first questions to me after reading it, however, was, "Dad, who is this for?" I paused and then replied, "It's for everyone who performs or cares about music." That was true, but only partially so. The pause was because I really wrote it for David— for someone who I knew could be persuaded by the evidence and who would genuinely care about the results. I hope that will be true of many readers, but David was my archetype, and so it is to him that this book is affectionately dedicated.

*How
Equal Temperament
Ruined Harmony*

Prelude

One must remember that the voluminous literature about tuning systems in the past comes from people who were of no musical importance.

E. MICHAEL FREDERICK, "Some Thoughts on Equal Temperament Tuning"[1]

THE AUDIENCE HUNG on every word uttered by the silver-maned maestro. As he spoke, heads nodded slowly all around the room in silent acknowledgment of the fundamental truths he imparted. For eighteen years Christoph von Dohnányi had led the Cleveland Orchestra, one of the premier ensembles in the world, and now he was reflecting on his tenure in a kind of "exit interview" with music critic Donald Rosenberg before four hundred–odd friends and admirers. Having recently returned from a final performance at Carnegie Hall, Dohnányi at one point mused about a frustration in the preparation of Beethoven's Ninth Symphony for that program. No recording exists of his remarks in that January twilight in 2002, but my recollection is that he said the following:

The symphony begins with about two minutes of a D-minor chord. But after that D minor comes a striking shift to B-flat major. In rehearsal, I just couldn't get that B-flat chord to sound right. I mean, I know what a major third is, and all of the players are consummate professionals, but we tried it over and over and I was never satisfied.

At that moment I knew I had to write this book. Here was one of the great conductors of the world, leader of one of the greatest orchestras in the world, and he didn't understand why this apparently simple shift in harmony from a D-minor to a B♭-major chord didn't sound right. If he didn't know, then it seemed logical to assume that most musicians wouldn't know. But I think I know. It's all wrapped up in recent evolutions in musical performance and teaching, the result of decades of delusion, convenience, ignorance, conditioning, and oblivion.

Does that sound harsh? Stay with me, gentle reader. It is not a reflection on the mastery of superb musicians like Christoph von Dohnányi, but by the end of this book, I hope you'll see that, contrary to the old adage, what most musicians don't know *has* hurt them, along with injuring the music they make.

NOT LONG AGO someone wrote a popular book on the history of musical temperament and concluded that Rameau discovered equal temperament (ET) in 1737, and basically we all lived happily ever after.[2] What a relief! Evolution to a more perfect state of being! Natural selection! Progress in scientific understanding! Now we can get on with making music, having solved that nasty conundrum of dividing the octave into twelve notes. If only musicians of the past had known this, how much better their music would have sounded! This is what most musicians think, and who can blame them? The standard scholarly study of the subject for the last half century, *Tuning and Temperament*, by Murray Barbour (1951), opined that much of Bach's organ music "would have been dreadfully dissonant in any sort of tuning except equal temperament"—not that Barbour had ever heard anything other than equal temperament when he wrote the book, as he once admitted.[3] In spite of his predisposition to favor ET, Barbour detailed about 150 historical tuning systems. Why so many? And why were people still experimenting even after they "discovered" ET?

Reconciling musical acoustics to a twelve-note division of the octave, as we use in our musical system, is an extremely difficult thing to do, and ET solved the problem in an efficient—one might almost say elegant—way. G♯ was the same note as A♭, of course. Any child studying piano could see that single black key between the G and the A. And composers like Schoenberg, active in the early part of the twentieth century, could write twelve-tone music in which the "spelling" of the notes in the harmony was irrelevant. Chords in tonal music traditionally had set ways of identifying the pitches—a C-minor triad, for example, had to be notated as C–E♭–G, not C–D♯–G—but with the newer styles of atonal music and twelve-tone music, it didn't matter, especially since ET had rendered the distinction academic.

Piano tuners have thus been tuning ET for decades now, and what pianos do, so do we all if we ever perform with one. Historically it used to be the organ's tuning that dictated where the notes were to be found in any given town, but we don't perform often enough with organs anymore, and, besides, organs—both pipe and electronic—have mostly been tuned to ET for decades anyway. So ET has been a given for generations of musicians through most of the twentieth century and into the twenty-first. They think in ET. They tune in ET. They hear in ET. Notes in ET are "in tune," and everything else is "out of tune."

It's time for that to change.

I hasten to point out that I didn't call this book "How Equal Temperament Ruined Music." I don't believe that. It's the sound of the music, the *harmony*, that has been compromised by the exclusive use of ET in performance. Modern musicians would disagree because they're used to it, and because it's convenient. But what I want to show in this book is that, first of all, in some respects ET doesn't sound as good as some of the alternatives. Second, I want to show that before the standardization of ET became so overwhelming that nobody got to hear anything else when they were growing up, musicians knew about ET and in many cases chose not to use it. If I succeed in doing those two things, then modern musicians will have to reconsider their exclusive use of ET for every kind of music. It's as simple as that. In the meantime I'll try to keep it short because every musician I know would rather be making music than reading about it any day.

CHAPTER ONE

Shouldn't Leading
Notes Lead?

*Upon such simple facts we might have supposed the musical scale to
be founded; but when we come to tune a pianoforte, and raise the
fifths one upon another, to our surprise we find the last note C, too
sharp for the C we set out with. This inexplicable difficulty no one
has attempted to solve; the Deity seems to have left music in an
unfinished state, to show his inscrutable power.*

WILLIAM GARDINER, *The Music of Nature* (1832)[1]

IF MODERN STRING PLAYERS are taught anything about
varying tuning from ET, they are taught that "leading notes
should lead." This approach is often attributed to the great cellist
Pablo Casals (1876–1973), who advocated what he called "expressive intonation." What that means in practical terms is that in a
common cadential progression involving a leading note, say G♯ to
A, the G♯ should be higher than its ET position so that it leads
more effectively to the resolution on A. Conversely, when a B♭
leads down to A, the B♭ should be lower to enhance that linear
progression and the inexorable pull toward the resolution. That
all sounds logical and makes some sense in the context of a single melodic line. But most musicmaking has a harmonic element
as well—the notes of the melody are part of a progression of
chords that accompany the melody—and that harmonic element
is not well served by that approach. In fact, not only should an

ascending leading note *not* be raised from its ET position, but a harmonic approach would dictate that it should be *lowered* from its ET position. Similarly the descending leading note—the B♭ going to A—should be *raised* to be better in tune. How can that possibly be so? And why should you believe me—an academic musician and nonentity in the music performance world—rather than a legendary player like Pablo Casals?

The answer lies in the science of musical acoustics, a branch of physics that deals with musical sounds and the relationships between them. This is something that cannot be fudged or changed. It is what it is.

Sound is created by vibrations. The musical pitch of sound is determined by the speed of those vibrations, which we measure by their "frequency" (number of vibrations per second of time). For example A=440, today's pitch standard, refers to a note vibrating at a frequency of 440 vibrations per second (a unit we call a hertz and abbreviate as Hz). We know that the simplest musical intervals have simple ratios in the relationship between their frequencies. The unison is the simplest: The frequency of a note has a 1:1 ratio with the frequency of another note at the identical pitch. That means that a unison sound consists of two notes vibrating at the identical frequency. The octave is the next simplest: The frequency of a note has a 2:1 ratio with that of a note an exact octave away. In fact a string of twice the length (assuming the same tension and mass per unit of length) will vibrate at half the frequency and thus sound an octave below the first string. Or a string of half the length will vibrate twice as fast and sound an octave higher. It works for wind instruments, too. A tube of half the length will sound an octave higher than a longer tube, and a tube of twice the length will sound an octave lower.

The reason these simple intervals are in such simple ratios to one another is because they are part of the acoustical phenomenon called the harmonic series, or overtone series. Any sound

What Is the Harmonic Series?

The harmonic series is an acoustical phenomenon consisting of a sequence of pitches that is related to a lower pitch. A sound having a frequency of, say, 100 vibrations per second (Hz) will also cause sounds to resonate in simple ratios with those 100 Hz, namely 200 Hz, 300 Hz, 400 Hz, and so on. These ratios, 2:1, 3:1, 4:1, are actually in an invariable harmonic relationship with the note at 100 Hz, or fundamental note, as it's called (see figure 1). The sequence of successive intervals is always octave (2:1), fifth (3:2), fourth (4:3), major third (5:4), minor third (6:5), two intervals between a minor third and a whole tone (7:6 and 8:7), large whole tone (9:8), small whole tone (10:9), and progressively smaller intervals *ad infinitum*. The semitone is said to begin in the sequence at 16:15—four octaves above the fundamental—but that interval can also be derived as the difference between a 5:4 pure major third and a 4:3 pure fourth (invert and multiply: $4/5 \times 4/3 = 16/15$).

Each note of the harmonic series is found at frequencies corresponding to multiples of the fundamental frequency. Basically any sound possesses all the notes in its harmonic series to varying degrees, and that variability is the reason the timbres of instruments playing the same pitch are different: their harmonics have different strengths. It is also thought that the prevalence of the octave, fifth, fourth, and major and minor thirds in the lower part of the harmonic series contributed to the development of our concept of harmony, in which those intervals form the most common components of chords. Chords in the Western (that is, European) music tradition, therefore, are not merely a culturally evolved arrangement of musical sounds into a system but a natural phenomenon based on the physical science of acoustics.

produced by natural means (rather than electronic, for example) has overtones—frequencies that sound in acoustical relationship to the note being sounded (which we call the fundamental pitch). In fact the distinctive timbre of a sound—like the difference between an oboe and a violin sound, for example—is created by the relative strength of these overtones, so they are a constant and critical part of music. The harmonic series goes on to an infinite number of overtones, well beyond human hearing. Figure 1 shows the first four octaves of the harmonic or overtone series for a fundamental note of C. Note that each overtone marked with an arrow is very approximate to our scale and is actually shaded in the direction of the arrow. Thus, as any baroque trumpet player at the mercy of the harmonic series could tell you, the two B♭s and the A are low; the F is high.

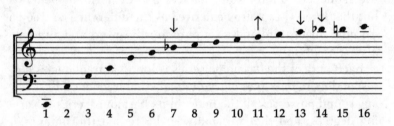

Figure 1. Harmonic Series.

   All these overtones (in addition to others farther up the harmonic series) are present, to a greater or lesser extent, whenever a note is sounded. Experience over many centuries has shown that when we make music together, we want our jointly sounding notes to have these fundamental acoustical relationships, especially at the bottom end of the harmonic series: if unisons are not exactly in a 1:1 ratio, and octaves are not exactly in a 2:1 ratio, then the intervals produced are slightly off in pitch and "disagree" musically in a noticeably dissonant way. That's what we call being out of tune. In fact nobody argues about the ratios for unisons and octaves: There

HOW EQUAL TEMPERAMENT RUINED HARMONY

is only one way for them to be in tune or out of tune. The situation changes already with the next simplest ratio, however.

The ratio for the fifth is 3:2, which means that a string or tube of 2/3 the length will sound a fifth higher in pitch than the longer one. Also, a string or tube of one and a half times the length will sound a fifth lower. As the next simplest ratio after the unison at 1:1 and the octave at 2:1, this acoustically pure fifth would also seem to be a desirable sonority, and in the Middle Ages, when fifths constituted the predominant harmonic interval, the 3:2 fifth was undoubtedly used all the time. We call such a system "Pythagorean tuning," after the Greek philosopher and mathematician Pythagoras, in deference to his supposed "discovery" of the 3:2 ratio in ancient times. But as our musical culture began to be based more and more on keyboard instruments with a twelve-note octave (our standard piano octave), musicians found that they couldn't use a consistent fifth that was absolutely pure. Let's find out why.

Figure 2. Circle of Fifths.

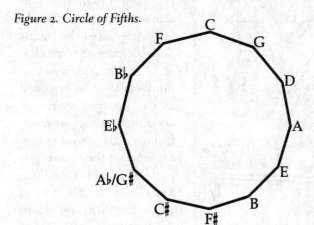

If you were to start at a very low note on the piano and tune acoustically pure fifths up from there, eventually you'd expect to get back to the note you started on. For example, starting on C, you would tune C–G–D–A–E–B–F♯–C♯–G♯ (that is, A♭)–E♭–B♭–

Pythagoras

Pythagoras, the Greek philosopher and religious teacher, lived in the second half of the sixth century B.C. He was born on Samos, an island near the coast of Turkey, and later emigrated to Croton, a Greek colony in southern Italy, where he established a religious order. He was then expelled from that city and settled in nearby Metapontum. A famous mathematician, he is best known today for the eponymous theorem concerning the squares of the sides of a right-angled triangle.

Pythagoras's musical significance lies in his supposed discovery of the numerical basis of acoustics. None of his writings survive, but it is said that he heard hammers of different weights striking a blacksmith's anvil and creating different musical intervals. He then discovered that musical consonances could be represented by ratios derived from the *tetractys* (1, 2, 3, 4), the sequence of numbers that he regarded as the mystical source of all things in the universe. In music 2:1 (and 4:2) corresponds to the octave; 3:1, to the octave plus the fifth; 4:1, to the double octave; 3:2, to the fifth; and 4:3, to the fourth (see also "What Is the Harmonic Series?").

Pythagoras experiments with musical ratios, from Franchino Gafurius's Theorica Musice *(1492).*

F–C. Twelve fifths should equal seven octaves and come back around the "circle" to C, as in figure 2.

This is what actually happens in ET. But twelve *acoustically pure* fifths don't make a nice neat circle like that. Look at the ratios. A pure fifth has the ratio 3:2, so if we compare twelve of them with seven 2:1 octaves (multiplying the ratios as we add the intervals), what do we get?

Note to mathophobes: This is not math, it's arithmetic.

$$\frac{3}{2} \times \frac{3}{2} \times \frac{3}{2} \times \frac{3}{2} \times \frac{3}{2} \times \frac{3}{2} \times \frac{3}{2} \times \frac{3}{2} \times \frac{3}{2} \times \frac{3}{2} \times \frac{3}{2} \times \frac{3}{2} = 129.746$$

$$\frac{2}{1} \times \frac{2}{1} \times \frac{2}{1} \times \frac{2}{1} \times \frac{2}{1} \times \frac{2}{1} \times \frac{2}{1} = 128.0$$

Figure 3. "Circle" of Pure Fifths.

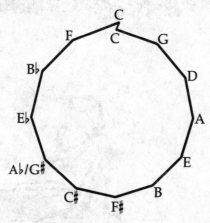

That twelfth fifth, the one we expect to complete the circle and bring us back to our starting note, actually overshoots the target pitch and puts us in a ratio of 129.746:128, or 1.014:1 instead of 1:1 (see figure 3). In musical terms, it puts us about a quarter of a semitone too high. That may not seem like much, but in fact it's an excruciating discrepancy called a "comma," which renders that note unusable as a substitute for a unison or octave. What

Pythagoras at the forge: inspiration strikes

can we do? We can tune eleven pure fifths and leave that last interval narrow so that it's not a 3:2 fifth but completes the circle. Or we can change the ratio of some or all the fifths in between, so that we arrive back at our original starting note. (Since the note of arrival is too high in pitch, we would need to make the accumulated intervals smaller.) ET is so elegant because it narrows—tempers—all the fifths ever so slightly (each by 1/12 of the overall discrepancy, or comma) and thus allows us to end the series of twelve fifths in tune with the starting pitch, as happens in figure 2.

The next simplest ratio after the 3:2 fifth is the 4:3 fourth. But there is nothing new in looking at the fourth, since it's simply the difference between a note's octave and fifth. So the problems of the fourth are the inverse of the problems of the fifth, and any narrowing of the fifth from its pure ratio must increase the size of the fourth by that same amount in order to complete the octave. Thus in tempering (narrowing) all the fifths by 1/12 of a comma, ET also widens the fourth by the same tiny amount in order to keep the octave at a 2:1 ratio. The story might end there—and for many modern writers and musicians it has—except that there is a terrible musical cost to fixing all the notes in this efficient way.

So convenient is this system that many musicians today don't notice how horrible the next important harmonic interval is in ET. The next simplest ratio after the 4:3 fourth belongs to the major third, at 5:4. The fifth and fourth of ET aren't bad, being out of acoustical purity by only about one-fiftieth of a semitone, but the major third is where ET fails the harmonic purity test. ET major thirds are extremely wide—about one-seventh of a semitone wider than acoustically pure 5:4 major thirds. That's about seven times the amount of discrepancy shown between ET fifths and acoustically pure fifths. This interval is the invisible elephant in our musical system today. Nobody notices how awful the major thirds are. Nobody comments. Nobody even recognizes that the

Ignoring the mammoth Major 3rd of ET

HOW EQUAL TEMPERAMENT RUINED HARMONY

elephant exists. Living with this elephant is assumed to be so much better than the unknown alternatives that it's a nonissue. Asked about it, some people even claim to prefer the elephant; they have grown to like elephantine thirds. But I'm here to shake those people out of their cozy state of denial. It's the acoustics, baby: Ya gotta feel the vibrations.

My late colleague Arthur H. Benade, one of the world's leading experts on musical acoustics, described an experiment he liked to perform with musicians in his lab:

> It is an easily verifiable fact that if one sets up the two oscillators to give a frequency ratio of 1.25992 (corresponding to an equal-temperament interval . . .), instead of our experimentally verified 1.25000 ($= 5/4$) ratio . . . , everyone notices the resulting beats, and all the musicians in the group will say that an out-of-tune (sharp) major third is being sounded. When I tell my experimenters that the . . . interval is the equal-temperament version of the major third, they typically react with skepticism or dismay. . . . They respond in even more intense fashion to the extremely rough-sounding combination whose frequency ratio is 1.26563 ($= 81/64$) . . . This particular ratio, which is the product of 2000-year-old arithmetical ingenuity, is called a Pythagorean third.
>
> When I sound the equal-temperament and Pythagorean major thirds by means of two electronic tone generators, the usual question is "What makes anyone think that those are acceptable tunings?"
>
> Arthur H. Benade, Fundamentals of Musical Acoustics (1976)[2]

Nothing can change the fact that the major third in ET is a long way from acoustical purity.* When notes are perfectly in tune, the sound of the interval they create is stable and tranquil.

---

*Since the ET major third is wide, the ET minor third must be commensurately narrow, because they both occupy the interval of the fifth. However, the ear seems to tolerate greater variance in the quality of the minor third.

When notes are slightly out of tune, even the tiniest amount, there is interference between the vibrations of the harmonic overtones of the two notes and we hear a pulsation, as Benade noted in his experiment, that we call "beats." Professional tuners know all about this and use it to their advantage. They know how fast the beats should be for an interval to be "in tune" in ET, whether it's the fifth from G to D, or the fifth from A to E a step higher which, because of the faster vibrations of higher pitches, will need to beat slightly faster (about 1.12 times) in order to be tempered the same amount. It's a subtle thing. But the major third of ET is so far out of tune that you can barely count the beats. Beating at nearly twelve times the speed of the fifth, it positively jangles.

No matter how masterful they are as musicians, many performers today don't hear how bad the ET major third is because it's what they're used to (conditioning) and because they've never heard an acoustically pure major third (ignorance). They're convinced that the ET major third must be the proper sound because it's what modern—and therefore obviously more enlightened—theorists have devised (delusion), and they wouldn't want to change because it would be too much trouble (convenience). Mostly, they don't want to think about it (oblivion).

As inconvenient as it may be, it's time for modern musicians to think about this and, where appropriate, make some changes.

CHAPTER TWO

How Temperament Started

Music came first, then the scales accrued after ages of experiment;
then came the theorists to explain them.

SIR PERCY BUCK, *Proceedings of the*
Musical Association (1940)[1]

THE EARLY HISTORY of temperament seems to date from
the 1400s, although the earliest practical discussions come from
the following century. As more thirds occurred in the harmonies
written by composers, musicians recognized the importance of
making them sound good in performance. That meant compromising the purity of the fifth—formerly the predominant interval—and making the newly predominant major thirds sound as
good as possible. Early on that often meant making the thirds
absolutely pure at 5:4. Unfortunately in a twelve-note octave, a
circle of pure major thirds is just as impossible as a circle of pure
fifths; so obviously not all thirds could be pure. (Three pure
major thirds = $5/4 \times 5/4 \times 5/4 = 125/64$, or 1.953:1 instead of 2:1 for
the octave.)

What Are Pure Intervals?

Pure intervals occur when the speed of the vibrations of two or more notes (that is, their frequencies) match the simple acoustical ratios of the harmonic series (see "What Is the Harmonic Series?" on page 21). For the most commonly used harmonic intervals, these ratios are as follows:

unison	1:1
octave	2:1
fifth	3:2
fourth	4:3
major third	5:4
minor third	6:5

For example, a note vibrating at a frequency of 400 times per second (Hz) would be an octave above a note vibrating at 200 Hz, and an octave below one vibrating at 800 Hz. It would be a fifth below a note vibrating at 600 Hz because 600:400 is the same as 3:2. It would be a fourth above a note vibrating at 300 Hz and a major third below a note vibrating at 500 Hz. Except for the octave, these intervals are not exactly the same size as those in equal temperament, but they are pure because they match the harmonic

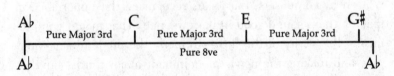

Figure 4. Three Pure Major Thirds Compared with an Octave.

That was mostly all right because Renaissance composers weren't using all the major thirds anyway. The most common temperament of the Renaissance was something called quarter-comma meantone, which had eight acoustically pure thirds and

ratios and because, when sounded together, they are completely *beatless*. That means that their sounds fit so perfectly together that there is no interference between their respective vibrations: Any variance from the exact ratio will cause a beat or pulsation— *waoo-waoo-waoo-waoo*—and the faster the pulsation, the less pure the interval must be. For example, two notes vibrating at 400 and 401 Hz, respectively, will pulse or beat once per second in addition to sounding the two frequencies; notes sounding together at 400 and 402 Hz will beat twice per second, and so on. Those intervals are not pure unisons because the frequencies of the notes are not exactly in a 1:1 ratio. (For a numerical chart showing the size of pure intervals in comparison with ET and other tunings systems, see the appendix.)

A musical system that calls for harmonically pure intervals at all times is called Just intonation. It requires that notes have the flexibility to vary in pitch according to the needs of the harmony at any given moment, and thus is only possible with voices or on instruments with the capacity to make real-time adjustments as the music is being performed.

four excruciating ones.* Still, not having B–D♯, D♭–F, F♯–A♯, etc. was not a huge handicap since Renaissance composers did not notate music with signatures of more than two flats, and rarely with any sharps at all. The real cost of this system was a fifth that was really not very pleasant but that became tolerable when heard with the perfectly euphonious third.

*These four intervals are really diminished fourths rather than major thirds anyway. A note tuned as G♯, for example, would make a diminished fourth with the C above it, creating a very dissonant interval as compared with an A♭–C pure third.

The reason that meantone demanded such narrow fifths is because of the relationship between the fifths and the major thirds in *any* system. We have already seen that tuning pure fifths or even ET fifths creates major thirds that are very much wider than pure. A series of four 3:2 fifths up from C, for example (C–G, G–D, D–A, A–E) causes us to arrive on a note E that is excruciatingly wide as a major third (81:64 instead of the pure ratio of 80:64 or 5:4—the 81:80 discrepancy being another kind of comma), as shown in the following diagram.

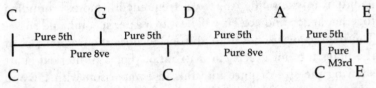

Figure 5. Four Pure Fifths Compared with Two Octaves Plus a Pure Major Third.

If instead we *start* with a 5:4 major third as the basis of the system, as is true of quarter-comma meantone, the four intervening fifths must all be narrow by quite a lot since they "create" the major third: The narrower the fifths, the narrower the resulting major third. In order to achieve acoustically pure major thirds, four consecutive fifths in the "circle," in fact, must be tempered (narrowed) by one-quarter of the comma difference between Pythagorean and pure major thirds; hence the terminology "quarter-comma meantone." The whole tone in this system, by the way, is exactly half of the major third (made from two tempered fifths instead of four), so that's where the term "mean [that is, averaged] tone" comes from.* The resulting series of fifths, how-

---

*Actually, in quarter-comma meantone, the whole tone is also the average (mean) between the 9:8 and 10:9 major and minor tones of Just intonation, a system in which all intervals are pure. This makes sense because both Just and quarter-comma meantone use pure 5:4 major thirds, but Just achieves them by using one large and one small whole tone, whereas meantone has a single size

ever, comes up too short to make a circle, leaving the last "fifth" much too wide to be usable, as shown in figure 6. (This was called a "wolf" because it "howled" instead of sounding like a normal fifth, which of course it wasn't anyway, being rather a diminished sixth.) Like most meantone systems, the one shown in figure 6 is constructed roughly symmetrically around D, although the "wolf" was probably placed just as often between C♯ and A♭ as between G♯ and E♭. And it could have been moved even farther in one direction or the other in order to favor flat keys or sharp keys. The fact that all the rest of the fifths are the same size, however, means that such meantone systems are referred to as "regular" meantone systems.

Figure 6. Regular Meantone Fifth "Circle."

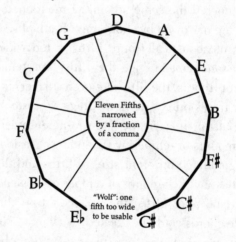

While this tuning system continued in common use in many places until around the end of the seventeenth century, already in

---

of whole tone that divides the major third in two, and simultaneously averages the two different sizes of whole tone in the Just system. Since other forms of meantone, like fifth- and sixth-comma systems, do not have a pure 5:4 major third, their whole tones are not an average of the two Just whole tones, although they are always one half of their respective major thirds, as they are in ET.

the sixteenth century some people were experimenting with variant systems. By reducing the amount of tempering—that is to say, by making the fifths slightly wider than in quarter-comma meantone (spreading the comma over five or six fifths instead of four)—they were able to make less differentiation between the four horrible thirds in the system and the eight good thirds. These latter weren't acoustically pure thirds any longer, but they were still pretty good, and the fifths were better. So while the standard Renaissance meantone system narrowed the fifths by one-quarter of a comma, some musicians found a one-fifth- or one-sixth-comma meantone to be more conducive to their needs.

Another type of temperament emerged when someone decided or discovered that all the fifths in a system didn't have to be tempered the same amount. I mentioned that in ET all the fifths are narrowed by about one-fiftieth of a semitone because a series of acoustically pure fifths is too wide. In the standard Renaissance meantone, the fifths are tempered by a larger amount (that is, the fifths are even smaller) in order to make the major thirds pure. The new "irregular" systems that began to be especially popular in the late seventeenth century mixed different amounts of tempering (including occasional wide fifths) and thus contained different sizes of fifths and thirds (see figure 7). By adjusting the amount of tempering as well as the mix of tempered and pure fifths, the wolf could be eliminated and more usable chords could be created.

This was especially useful as composers began writing more chromatic lines and complex harmonies, like diminished and seventh chords. Composers also began writing in a greater variety of keys, although still nothing like the number used in the nineteenth century.

While regular temperaments could always be "shaded" in the tuning process to favor one key or another (placing the wolf at some little-used interval in the key), some of the new irregular

Figure 7. Sample Irregular Temperament Fifth Circle.

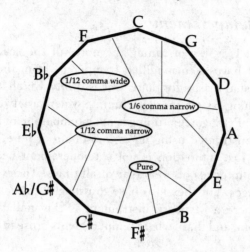

temperaments could actually be used in a wide range of signatures and keys without being adjusted. These were known almost interchangeably as "good temperaments," "well temperaments," or—if they could actually be used in any key without adjustment—as "circulating temperaments," meaning that they could be used in all the keys around the circle of fifths. It didn't mean that all the keys sounded the same, but at least they were all usable, some sounding better than others.

It is absolutely amazing that there were so many varieties of these irregular temperaments described and recommended by theorists, but it's because there was no obvious solution to the temperament problem. Each system had its advantages and disadvantages, had chords and keys that it favored and others that didn't sound so good, was easy to tune but didn't sound so great, or sounded quite good but was difficult to tune. These are the tuning systems by Andreas Werckmeister, Johann Philipp Kirnberger, Johann Georg Neidhardt, and Francesc'Antonio Vallotti, among others, whose names are famous in the tuning world. They became exceptionally popular as keyboard tuning systems

What Is Temperament?

Temperament is a way of tuning the notes of the scale using intervals that have been modified (tempered) from their pure forms. The usual reason for doing this is utility, which is to say, to make a tuning system more useful in a wider variety of musical situations. Pythagorean tuning is not a temperament because its scale is constructed using notes in a chain of pure, untempered fifths. Just intonation is not a temperament because it calls for pure intervals of every type at all times. These systems have advantages, but they also have drawbacks, particularly in situations where a keyboard instrument is the model for the musical system, and that's where temperaments arose in the first place.

ET is a temperament because its fifths are narrowed very slightly from the acoustically pure ratio of 3:2, so that twelve ET fifths in sequence arrive at a note that is seven octaves above the starting note, creating, at the same time, a scale where all twelve notes in the octave are equidistant (see "What Is an Octave Division?" on page 55). Its great advantage is that it is universally usable: It can be used in every key with identical musical effect. Its drawback is that its major third is much, much wider than an acoustically pure major third, and sounds quite harsh. That's one of the main reasons that other temperaments were more popular than ET throughout history: Musicians were not willing to tolerate thirds that were so dissonant.

Typically temperaments tried to balance euphony with utility—to have the most common chords and keys sound good at the expense of the least common chords and keys. To achieve that they usually tempered some fifths more than in ET (that is, made them narrower) while others were wider than in ET— often pure, in fact. A temperament in which all of the tempered fifths are the same size is called a regular temperament (see figure 6), and one in which fifths are of different sizes is called an irregular temperament (see figure 7). The most common regular temperament, of course, is ET, where the notes of the scale are created by tempering equally each of the twelve fifths. It is possible to create equally tempered systems that use more (or less) than twelve notes in the octave by tempering the "fifths" a different amount, such that a certain number of them in sequence eventually comes back to the starting note (see also "What Is an Octave Division?").

Other well-known regular temperaments include the quarter-comma, fifth-comma, sixth-comma (and so on), meantone temperaments, in which all the fifths but one are tempered the same amount (see figure 6). They are called meantone because the whole tone is exactly one-half the size (that is, the "mean") of the major third. Extended meantone temperaments are systems in which the major and minor semitones within a whole tone are all usable: in which, for example, the separate pitches of both G♯ and A♭ are available to the performer (see figure 10). Such systems are possible only on instruments that can vary the position of the notes as needed for the harmony, or on split keyboards with more than twelve notes to the octave.

because, typically combining pure fifths with tempered fifths, they were easier for keyboard players to tune (in an age when harpsichords had to be tuned daily and only noblemen could afford a professional tuner), and because they were serviceable in a wide variety of keys.

This is the kind of system Johann Sebastian Bach intended for the preludes and fugues of his *Well-Tempered Clavier*. Sometimes you will see Bach's term, *wohltemperirt*, translated as "equal tempered," but that's not what it referred to, and it's not what Bach meant. Irregular temperaments, even those that could be classified as circulating temperaments, have a lot of different sizes of each interval. For example, in Vallotti's system, there are six differents sizes of semitone and three different sizes of whole tone. Combinations of those basic intervals mean that there is also a wide variety of major and minor thirds. So chords that depend on those thirds can sound very different within the same temperament. This creates a tremendous diversity in the way different keys sound in these irregular temperaments, and that was one of the things that musicians of the time liked about them.

By Bach's time (1685–1750), musicians had long known about ET. There are unequivocal discussions of it by around 1640, if not earlier, but still theorists continued to try to find other ways of tuning, and musicians preferred not to use it.

> The octave being always divided into five tones and two limmas [diatonic semitones]; by increasing the tones equally till each becomes double the diminishing limma, . . . the diesis, or difference between the major and minor limma, will be contracted to nothing, which . . . annihilates all the false consonances. But the harmony in this system of 12 Hemitones is extremely coarse and disagreeable.
>
> Robert Smith, *Harmonics, or the Philosophy of Musical Sounds* (1759)[2]

Smith described ET as a widening of the whole tone over that of meantone, at the same time as the difference between the

A serious temperament discussion

Robert Smith

Robert Smith, the English mathematician, was christened at Lea, Lincolnshire, on October 16, 1689, and died in Cambridge in 1768. He entered Trinity College, Cambridge, in 1708, became a senior fellow in 1739, and master in 1742; he was also a fellow of the Royal Society and Plumian Professor of Astronomy (1716–60), succeeding his brilliant cousin, Roger Cotes, who had edited the second edition of Newton's *Principia* and who died at thirty-four. Smith also served as Master of Mechanics to King George II.

An amateur cellist, Smith published his book on musical acoustics, *Harmonics, or the Philosophy of Musical Sounds*, in Cambridge in 1749, then revised and enlarged it for London publication in 1759. He also wrote *Postscript . . . upon the Changeable Harpsichord* (London, 1762). Smith was one of the first writers to give actual beat rates for the intervals of a musical system, though in doing so, he also had to provide a selection of performance frequencies, since beat rates rise with the pitch, and there was no standard at the time. His preferred temperament was one he called the "System of Equal Harmony"—not ET, but rather a system in which the intervals of the fifth and the major sixth from the same starting note beat at the same rate. It was similar in effect to meantone and corresponds roughly to a

major and minor semitone is erased. He recognized that such a system removes the "false consonances," where G♯ is forced to serve for A♭, for example, but he still disdains the result from a harmonic standpoint. "Extremely coarse and disagreeable" harmony is not the only reason that musicians avoided ET, however. Johann Georg Neidhardt, a theorist whom Bach knew, said of it in 1732:

50-division system (see "What Is an Octave Division?" on page 55). The eighteenth-century music historian John Hawkins reported that Smith was assisted in his beat-counting technology by John Harrison, the clockmaker whose story was told in Dava Sobel's book *Longitude* (New York, 1995). In his scientific approach to music, Smith anticipated Helmholtz, who, however, does not seem to have known his work on music, even though he was well acquainted with Smith's earlier book, *A Compleat System of Opticks* (Cambridge, 1738).

Robert Smith, *portrait by John Vanderbank (1730), Trinity College, Cambridge.*

On his death Smith made various bequests to Cambridge, including money for two highly prestigious prizes in mathematics and natural philosophy, the "Smith's Prizes," which have been given annually ever since, honoring along the way such luminaries as Lord Kelvin, James Clerk Maxwell, and Alan Turing.

Most people do not find in this tuning that which they seek. It lacks, they say, variety in the beating of its major 3rds and, consequently, a heightening of emotion. In a triad everything sounds bad enough; but if the major 3rds alone, or minor 3rds alone, are played, the former sound much too high, the latter much too low.

Johann Georg Neidhardt, *Gäntzlich erschöpfte, mathematische Abteilungen des diatonisch-chromatischen, temperirten Canonis Monochordi* (1732)[3]

Along with criticizing the thirds as too far from pure, Neid-hardt complained that ET's uniform intervals lack expressive variety. Indeed, Bach's *Well-Tempered Clavier* was not written to demonstrate the superiority of ET, as is often claimed. It wasn't even written for ET, but for an irregular temperament that worked in a wide variety of keys. Such a temperament was convenient, yes, because the player didn't have to retune all the time as the keys changed (as would have been necessary with a regular meantone system), but its irregularity also meant that the flavor of the chords was slightly different in each key, and the character of each key was thus slightly different. It is no accident that this was the era when descriptions of key characteristics really came into their own. For example, B♭ major, according to one writer (Francesco Galeazzi, 1796), was "tender, soft, sweet, effeminate, fit to express transports of love, charm, and grace," while E major was "very piercing, shrill, youthful, narrow, and somewhat harsh." But B♭ major was not only at a different pitch from E major in irregular temperaments, their scales and their harmonies were completely different. The issue of key characteristics will come up again later.

Carl Philipp Emanuel Bach, J. S. Bach's second son, is often said to have favored ET explicitly, and his supposed preference is sometimes used, by implication, to stand for the preferences of his father. For example, the famed acoustician Hermann von Helmholtz wrote in 1863, "Sebastian's son, Emanuel, who was a celebrated pianist, and published in 1753 a work of great authority in its day 'on the true art of playing the pianoforte,' requires this instrument to be always tuned in equal temperament."[4] Sometimes C. P. E. Bach's younger contemporary Friedrich Wilhelm Marpurg is cited as a witness to Bach's preference for ET. Yet C. P. E. Bach's own prescription for a temperament calls for "most of the fifths" ("*den meisten Quinten*")[5] to be narrowed a very small amount, so that all keys would be usable. Having all the keys usable is certainly a characteristic of ET, but what is striking about C. P. E. Bach's description is that the defining feature of ET is that *all* the fifths are narrowed equally; so, allowing some of them (that is, all minus "most") by implication to remain wider than that, leaves open the possibility—nay, rather, the requirement—that C. P. E. Bach's tuning was circulating but unequal.* If this was true for the son, we can play the implication game in reverse and refute the use of ET by the father. More on J. S. Bach and his "well temperament" later.

---

*Moreover, J. S. Bach's youngest son, Johann Christian Bach (the so-called London Bach), became agent for the immigrant pianoforte maker Johannes Zumpe, and one of Zumpe's 1766 pianos—now in the Württembergisches Landesmuseum in Stuttgart—survives with split-key accidentals. It should be evident from the discussion in chapter three that this favors an extended meantone system. At least it is impossible to argue that seventeen keys to the octave is intended for ET.

CHAPTER THREE

Non-Keyboard Tuning

"Temperaments" are closed systems designed to help make the into-
nation of instruments with immovable pitch (like the organ and
harpsichord) convincing. But singers and players of stringed and
wind instruments have no such limitations—"temperament" is too
rigid a concept to apply to them.

BRUCE HAYNES, "Beyond Temperament: Non-Keyboard
Intonation in the 17th and 18th Centuries" (1991)[1]

MOST OF THE INK spilled over the issue of tuning and
temperament today, as well as in earlier centuries, has revolved
around the tuning of keyboard instruments—so much so that
nowadays we tend to think of the issue only in those terms. Even
within the historical performance community, musicians argue,
first of all, for the use of historical temperaments over ET, then
argue about which system by Werckmeister, Neidhardt, Kirnberger, Vallotti, or a host of other theorists is the appropriate system for the music at hand. But in contemplating the dozens of
different historical solutions, it's tempting to regard the situation
back then—and by extension the musicians as well—as hopelessly
confused. That view is not supported by the facts.

Toward the end of Bach's lifetime, at the same time that keyboard players seemed to be moving more and more toward serviceable irregular temperaments like Vallotti, non-keyboard performers

—strings, winds, and voices—were following a separate track. Oh, certainly, when they had to perform with a keyboard instrument, they undoubtedly did their best to be in tune with it, but they didn't stop recognizing where the notes *ought* to be, as opposed to where the keyboard notes were placed through the compromise of temperament. This is because the "dirty little secret" even of circulating temperaments like Vallotti is that, although the keys might all be usable, and the contrast between them creates a pleasing variety, some of them just don't sound very good. One clear piece of graphic evidence that non-keyboard players were not compromising the position of the sharps and flats is the violin fingerboard given by the French/English theorist, Peter Prelleur, in his 1730–31 treatise, *The Modern Musick-Master*. Notice in figure 8 how Prelleur shows the relative position of the notes on the fingerboard, and—wonder of wonders—A♭ is higher in pitch than G♯. If you look at the top of the diagram, you see the nut (the endpoint on which the strings rest on their way to the tuning pegs) and the pitches of the open strings: G, D, A, and E. Below them are G♯, D♯, A♯, and E♯, followed by A♭, E♭, B♭, and F. Since the sharped notes are closer to the nut—the open strings—they are all lower in pitch

Figure 8. Fingerboard Diagram. Peter Prelleur, The Modern Musick-Master (1730–31), "The Art of Playing on the Violin," between pp. 4 and 5.

than the flatted notes in the same position. There is no question about it, even though it's completely opposite from the "leading notes should lead" philosophy. Why is this so?

Consider the major thirds E–G♯ and A♭–C. If you think about the fact that the pure major third is narrower than the ET major third, that suggests that a E–G♯ third that is closer to being pure—even if not actually pure—is bound to have a lower G♯ in relation to E than would be the case in ET. Similarly an A♭–C major third, if narrower than in ET, would have a higher A♭ in relation to C as an A♭–C third against that same C in ET. Thus the G♯ is lower than in ET, and the A♭ is higher. But why did non-keyboard players do this instead of just placing the notes wherever the keyboard's temperament put them?

In the first place and most important, it was because they knew where the notes were *supposed* to be. They recognized keyboard temperament as a compromise that allowed the keyboard to play in a variety of keys—maybe even *all* the keys—but they also knew that some intervals didn't sound very good. Not being limited to twelve unchangeable notes to the octave, string players, wind players, and singers didn't have to make that compromise. If the score said A♭, they could play or sing A♭—not G♯ and not some compromise pitch halfway between the two. Aside from Prelleur's fingerboard, how do we know they did this?

One of the greatest and most influential singing teachers of the eighteenth century was Pier Francesco Tosi, whose treatise on singing, *Opinioni de' Cantori* (Bologna, 1723), was translated into English, German, and Dutch and reprinted for decades after its first appearance. In speaking of the singing master's responsibility to the student, Tosi says:

> He ought to make him sing the semitones according to the true rules. Not everyone understands that there is a major semitone and a minor semitone, because the difference cannot be demonstrated

Peter Prelleur

Peter Prelleur, composer, organist, and harpsichordist, was born probably in London in December 1705 to French immigrant parents, and died there on June 25, 1741. As a young man, he played the harpsichord at the Angel & Crown tavern in Whitechapel in east London, before securing the post of organist at the church of Saint Alban Wood Street, near Guildhall, in 1728. When Goodman's Fields Theatre opened on October 31, 1729, he was hired to play harpsichord, compose music, and arrange ballad operas—capitalizing on the success of John Gay's *The Beggar's Opera* in 1728. After that theater was suppressed in 1737, he continued as a theatrical composer and musician at the New Wells Theatre nearby. In March 1736 he was also elected in a bitter competition to become the first organist of Christ Church, Spitalfields, where he seems to have worked earlier in his life.

Harpsichordist (Prelleur?), from The Modern Musick-Master *(1730–31).*

Prelleur was one of the original signatories to the Royal Society of Musicians on August 28, 1739. His reputation is based primarily on his treatise, *The Modern Musick-Master, or The Universal Musician* (London, 1730–31), a "curiously adorn'd" book that contains instructions for singing, playing violin, flute, oboe, recorder, and harpsichord, as well as a history of music and a musical dictionary.

Pier Francesco Tosi

Pier Francesco Tosi was born at Cesena, near Ravenna, on August 13, 1654, and died at the nearby town of Faenza around July 16, 1732. He was a castrato singer, teacher, composer, and author of a very influential treatise on singing: *Opinioni de' Cantori Antichi e Moderni* (Bologna, 1723). As a young man, Tosi sang in a Rome church; then, after becoming a priest, in the Milan Cathedral choir from 1681 until his dismissal for misbehavior in 1685. His only known appearance in opera took place at Reggio nell'Emilia in 1687. After working in Genoa for a time, he left Italy in 1693 for London, where he taught and gave weekly performances. In

A singer, from Prelleur's Modern Musick-Master *(1730–31).*

the early eighteenth century he traveled widely on both musical and diplomatic missions for the Holy Roman Emperor Joseph I (died 1711) and the Elector Palatine. By 1724, he was again teaching in London but, after a few years, retired to Italy.

Tosi's singing treatise was a central authority on the topic for decades. A Dutch translation was published in Leiden in 1731, an English translation in London in 1743, and a much-expanded German version was issued by Johann Friedrich Agricola in Berlin in 1757, under the title *Anleitung zur Singkunst*.

on an organ or harpsichord if it doesn't have split keys. A whole tone is divided into nine almost imperceptible intervals which are called commas, five of which constitute the major semitone, and four the minor semitone. . . . An understanding of this matter has become very necessary, for if a soprano, for example, sings D♯ at the same pitch as E♭, a sensitive ear will hear that it is out of tune, since the latter pitch should be somewhat higher than the former.

Pier Francesco Tosi, Opinioni de' Cantori (1723)[2]

Tosi points out, first of all, that keyboards are unable to distinguish the two sizes of semitone unless they have "split keys"—"black notes" on the keyboard that are actually divided front-to-back in order to make available the two different notes at that one place on the keyboard. By the eighteenth century such split keys were pretty rare, so this option was not normally available. Tosi then remarks that a whole tone is divided into nine commas, with five of them making up the major semitone and four of them making up the minor semitone. Each whole tone obviously cannot be divided in two, since it consists of nine equal parts, so it must be made up of one major semitone (five commas) and one minor semitone (four commas). Tosi doesn't specify one division or the other and, depending on the key signature and the accidentals, either is possible. The essential point, made clear from Tosi's discussion elsewhere, is that the major semitone is the diatonic half-step (E–F, B–C, D–E♭, F♯–G, etc.) and the minor semitone is the chromatic half step (C–C♯, B♭–B, etc.). Thus, as in Prelleur's fingerboard diagram, a diatonic or scalar half step, like G♯–A, would be a major semitone and therefore larger than A♭–A, the chromatic and therefore minor half step. A singer would thus place either G♯ or A♭ as the proper semitone between G and A according to the key and the context (see figure 9).

One other interesting aspect of Tosi's discussion is that it gives us quite a clear picture of the amount of tempering he considered

What Are Major and Minor Semitones?

Major and minor semitones refer to small intervals within the whole tone in nonequal tuning systems. In ET, G♯ and A♭, for example, are the same note, so the distance from G to G♯ is the same as the distance from G to A♭, and G♯ to A, and A♭ to A, and so on. In other systems, however, G♯ and A♭ are different pitches, so the distance from G (and from A) to each of those intermediate notes is larger or smaller, depending on the way the tuning system is constructed.

In Pythagorean tuning and "expressive intonation," where the upward leading notes are high and the major thirds are wide, the sharped notes are higher than they are in ET, and the flatted notes are lower. Thus, the distance from G to G♯ would be greater than the distance from G♯ to A (because the G♯ is leading upward), and the distance from G to A♭ would be less than the distance from A♭ to A (because the A♭ is leading downward). The larger intervals in those cases—the chromatic semitones within one pitch name, like G to G♯ or A♭ to A—would be major semitones and the smaller ones, minor semitones.

In meantone-based systems, on the other hand, the situation is reversed: Leading notes are lower and flats are higher, so the diatonic semitone—between one pitch name and the next, like G♯ to A or G to A♭—is always the major semitone, while the chromatic semitone is smaller and therefore minor (see figure 9). Modern keyboard instruments with twelve notes to the octave are committed to one single version of the "accidental." That could mean equally spaced notes as in ET, or it could mean a higher or lower accidental depending on the tuning system, thus creating one major and one minor semitone within the whole tone. Keyboards with split keys—with more than twelve notes to the octave—provide the luxury of both chromatic versions of the note to the player, allowing, in this case, G to G♯, G to A♭, G♯ to A, and A♭ to A. Non-keyboard instruments usually have the flexibility to play whichever version of the note is called for in the score.

standard. If the whole tone has nine commas and the major semi-tone has five commas, then the octave may be calculated to have fifty-five commas. A major scale, for example, has five whole tones and two major (diatonic) semitones: tone-tone-semitone-tone-tone-tone-semitone. Five whole tones contain $5 \times 9 = 45$ commas, and two major semitones contain $2 \times 5 = 10$ commas, so an octave consists of $45 + 10 = 55$ commas. Some eighteenth-century tuning theorists actually talk about this "55-division" of the octave as practiced by "ordinary" musicians, so we know it was common. It also tells us that Tosi and his colleagues were tempering their fifths by about one-sixth of a comma, since that is the only system that corresponds to the 55-division of the octave. *

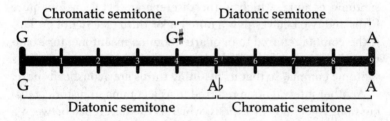

Figure 9. *Sample Nine-Comma Whole Tone Within the 55-Division Octave.*

Tosi's system differs from the regular sixth-comma keyboard temperament in that, as shown in figure 10, it is not limited to twelve notes to the octave. Again centered on D, the pattern would theoretically carry on for fifty-five notes, as the sequence of tempered fifths and resulting good thirds extended in each direction until they ultimately met back at the starting point, but this graphic shows the twenty-one most commonly used notes.

* The fifth of the 55-division system consists of 32 commas (three tones = 3×9 = 27 commas, plus one diatonic semitone = 5 commas), or 32/55 of an octave, which is almost precisely the same size as the interval achieved by narrowing the pure fifth by one-sixth of a comma.

What Is a Comma?

Commas are discrepancies. Tuning discussions from earlier centuries tend to toss around the word "comma" as if it were a single, fixed interval, but there are actually different discrepancies that theorists refer to when they use the word. There are two main commas. The first is the Pythagorean comma (also called the ditonic comma), which is the discrepancy between twelve pure fifths and seven pure octaves (see figure 3). That's the comma used in ET, where each of the twelve fifths is narrowed by one twelfth of the Pythagorean comma, creating an octave of twelve equally spaced notes.

The other discrepancy often used in tuning discussions is the syntonic comma, which is the discrepancy between four pure fifths and two octaves plus a pure major third (see figure 5). This is the comma referred to in quarter-comma meantone, for example, where each of the fifths is narrowed by one-quarter of the syntonic comma, so that its resulting thirds are acoustically pure.

Another interval often referred to as a comma in historical discussions is technically a *diesis*, which is the difference between a major semitone and a minor semitone (see "What Is an Octave Division?"). This tiny interval can vary according to the amount of tempering used in the fifths. Quarter-comma meantone, for example, has a larger diesis than sixth-comma meantone: The greater the tempering of the fifths ($1/4$ is greater than $1/6$, so its fifths are tempered more), the greater the difference between major and minor semitones, and the larger the diesis.

Last, commas are historically used to describe very small intervals in general, as in the individual units of octave division systems (see "What Is an Octave Division?").

What Is an Octave Division?

Octave divisions are tuning systems created by dividing the octave into a certain number of equal parts. ET is an octave division system, because its twelve equally tempered fifths also happen to divide the octave into twelve equal parts (see "What Is the Harmonic Series?" on page 21). You can see, however, that if you were not tied to a modern keyboard with its twelve notes per octave, it would be possible to divide the interval of the octave mathematically into any number of equal parts and make a musical system based on that division. The contemporary composer Easley Blackwood has demonstrated that principle with his Microtonal Études for divisions of thirteen up to twenty-four notes to the octave. Those pieces are available on CD: Cedille CDR 90000 018 (1994).

Some octave division systems were discussed in earlier centuries, too, especially because of their relationship to established temperaments. The 19-division system actually corresponds with extended third-comma meantone, since the intervals created in the division correspond with those of third-comma meantone. The same is true for 31-division and quarter-comma meantone, 43-division and fifth-comma meantone, and 55-division and sixth-comma meantone. Theorists (including Isaac Newton) also discussed the 53-division of the octave because of its close approximation to Just intonation (see "What Are Pure Intervals?" on page 32). Historically, theorists often referred to the individual units of octave division systems as commas (see "What Is a Comma?").

It's interesting to note that the regular sixth-comma meantone and the 55-division (or extended sixth-comma meantone) both result in a major third that is almost exactly halfway between an ET major third and an acoustically pure major third. I'll come back to Tosi's 55-division later.

Figure 10. Extended Meantone Fifth "Spiral."

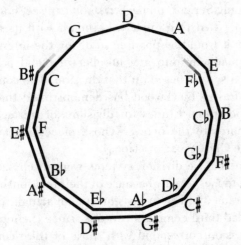

Among instrumentalists, two of the best witnesses from the middle of the eighteenth century—around the time of Bach's death—are Leopold Mozart and Johann Joachim Quantz.

Leopold Mozart is mostly known today as the grouchy and overprotective father of one of the world's greatest musical geniuses. In Leopold's own day, his fame rested largely on his *Treatise on the Fundamental Principles of Violin Playing*, published in 1756, the year of Wolfgang's birth. Even today this treatise has caused him to be regarded, not just as Wolfgang's father but as the father of modern violin playing.

In discussing chromatic scales on the violin, Leopold reminds his readers that:

. . . according to their proper ratios, notes with flat signs are a comma higher than those in the same position with a sharp sign. For example, D♭ is higher than C♯, A♭ higher than G♯, G♭ than F♯, and so on.

Leopold Mozart, Versuch einer gründlichen Violinschule (1756)[3]

To borrow a phrase from another musical context, that is "as clear as a button in the well water."[4] Notes with flat signs, like A♭, E♭, B♭, etc., are actually a little bit—one comma—higher than the corresponding sharp notes in the same position (G♯, D♯, A♯). This again corroborates what Prelleur had shown twenty-five years before in his fingerboard diagram, confirms the differentiation of semitones cited by Tosi, and demonstrates that the same kind of tuning principles were understood by Europe's finest and most influential musicians, even after the middle of the eighteenth century. And this is undoubtedly what Wolfgang learned at his father's knee when he began violin studies at the age of—oh, about eighteen months. (Actually Wolfgang seems not to have played violin seriously until he was about six, having focused until then on the keyboard. More about Wolfgang later.)

Johann Joachim Quantz was a fascinating figure. One of the greatest flute virtuosos of his day, he was also an influential theorist and teacher, his most famous pupil being Frederick the Great of Prussia. Quantz's *On Playing the Flute* (Berlin, 1752) deals not only with the technique of playing the flute but with matters of style and accompaniment. He also offers words of wisdom for musicians in general, among which is the following statement:

> A keyboard player who understands the division of the whole tone, also understands that D♯ and E♭ are differentiated by a comma, and therefore cause, because of its lack of split keys, some inequality of intonation upon this instrument [that is, the key-

Leopold Mozart

Leopold Mozart was born in Augsburg on November 14, 1719, and died in Salzburg on May 28, 1787. The son of a bookbinder, he was an actor, singer, and organist in his early years before concentrating on violin. In 1737, Leopold turned his back on the family business and entered Salzburg Benedictine University, studying philosophy and law. He received his bachelor's degree the next year, but by September 1739 he was expelled for poor attendance and a bad attitude. Following that, he became a musician to the Count of Thurn-Valsassina and Taxis in Regensburg. In 1743, Leopold was appointed fourth violinist in the court orchestra of Archbishop Firmian in Salzburg, the city that became his home for the rest of his life. In 1756, the same year as Wolfgang's birth, he published his important treatise on violin playing, *Versuch einer gründlichen Violinschule*. Even before its publication, however, Mozart was already well known. His works, including symphonies, concertos, and chamber and sacred music, circulated widely in German-speaking Europe and, in 1755, Lorenz Mizler petitioned—though unsuccessfully—for Mozart's membership in the Societät der Musicalischen Wissenschaften in Leipzig. By 1758 Mozart had advanced to the post of second violinist at Salzburg, and in 1763 to deputy *Kapellmeister*. Much of his later life was spent fretting over Wolfgang's career.

---

board] as compared with other instruments on which these notes are produced in their true ratios.

Johann Joachim Quantz, *Versuch einer Anweisung
die Flöte traversiere zu spielen* (1752)[5]

This corroborates Tosi's and Leopold Mozart's comments above. Quantz also provided a fingering chart for the flute. It's fascinating (though by this time perhaps not surprising) that he gives alternative fingerings for sharped and flatted notes on the

Leopold Mozart seems to have been arrogant, fussy, and occasionally pigheaded. The composer Johann Adolf Hasse once described him as "equally discontented everywhere," although he also acknowledged Leopold's crucial role in nurturing Wolfgang's talent. His voluminous correspondence reveals a father who loved his son but who was often frustrated in his attempts to help the world see the extent of his genius ("Oh yeah, right, Leo, and my kid's another Michelangelo").

Leopold Mozart, from Versuch einer gründlichen Violinschule (1756), *fig.* 2.

instrument. Where there is differentiation, the sharped notes are always demonstrably lower in pitch than the flatted ones. Quantz is not the only woodwind theorist to provide such alternative fingerings, of course.

In my view, however, Quantz's most striking contribution to the strength of this tuning tradition came in his capacity as an instrument designer. Since the late seventeenth century the flute had been made with a single key, operated by the little finger of

Semitone practice in the Mozart household

HOW EQUAL TEMPERAMENT RUINED HARMONY

the right hand near the bottom of the instrument. Because it opened rather than closed a hole like most woodwind keys, that single key served to raise the pitch of the lowest note of the flute by one semitone, from D to E♭. That's the way flutes were made by all the great makers of the baroque era, from Hotteterre to Rottenburgh to Bressan and even Grenser in his early years. Quantz decided in 1726 to add a second key. This seems, in retrospect, like a logical thing to do. The one-key flute can be enormously expressive, but one of its special characteristics is a difference in timbre, or tone color, in notes that use so-called forked fingerings (where one tone hole is left open and another lower down the instrument is covered). In the hands of an expert player these notes actually give an expressive color. More keys, however, could possibly make some of the notes play with a more consistent tone without awkward forked fingerings—something that would no doubt please the burgeoning amateur flute market. By the end of the eighteenth century, in fact, four- and six-key models, which attempted to address the tone consistency problems of the one-key flute, were in common use. But the key that Quantz decided to add to the one-key standard was at the bottom of the instrument, right next to the one that was already there. Quantz decided that the most crucial second key was one that would allow the player to play D♯ in addition to E♭ at the bottom of the instrument! As he explains in his 1752 treatise:

> The large semitone has five commas, the small one only four. Therefore E♭ must be a comma higher than D♯. If there were only one key on the flute, both the E♭ and the D♯ would have to be tempered as on the keyboard, where they are struck on a single key so that neither the E♭ to B♭ fifth nor the D♯ to B major third would sound truly. To mark this difference and to stop the notes in their proper proportions, it was necessary to add another key to the flute. . . . It is true that this distinction cannot be made on the keyboard where each pair of notes . . . is struck with a single key, and

Johann Joachim Quantz

Johann Joachim Quantz, the composer, theorist, and flute maker, was born near Hannover on January 30, 1697, and died at Potsdam on July 12, 1773. The son of a blacksmith, his first music lessons, in 1708, were with an uncle who was a town musician in Merseburg. During those early years Quantz became proficient on most of the orchestral instruments of the period, including

Johann Joachim Quantz, engraving by J. Schleuen.

the violin family, oboe, and trumpet. In March 1716 he accepted an invitation to join the Dresden town band, but then spent part of 1717 in Vienna studying counterpoint with Jan Dismas Zelenka. In 1718, back in Dresden, he became oboist in the Polish chapel of Augustus II, Elector of Saxony and king of Poland, but because he saw more possibilities as a flutist, he switched to the transverse flute in 1719 and took some lessons with the celebrated French player Pierre-Gabriel Buffardin. Quantz, however,

recourse must be made to tempering [that is, using a compromise position of the note as part of an irregular temperament]. Nevertheless, since the distinction is based on the nature of the notes, and since singers and string players can observe it without difficulty, it may be reasonably introduced on the flute.

Johann Joachim Quantz, *Versuch einer Anweisung die Flöte traversiere zu spielen* (1752)[6] regarded Dresden's leading violinist, Johann Georg Pisendel, as his foremost mentor in both performance and composition, especially in the blending of French and Italian styles.

Between 1724 and 1727 he studied counterpoint with Francesco Gasparini in Rome, impressed Alessandro Scarlatti, and met, among many others, the future Dresden *Kapellmeister* Johann Adolf Hasse. From summer 1726 to spring 1727 he visited Paris. In May 1728 Quantz, Pisendel, Buffardin, and others from the Dresden court accompanied their patron on a state visit to Berlin. There, Quantz made a very strong impression on the musical Prince Frederick and began twice-yearly visits to give him lessons on the flute.

When Frederick became king of Prussia in 1740, he offered Quantz 250 percent of his Dresden salary, release from duties in the opera orchestra, and an agreement to answer only to the monarch himself. With those incentives Quantz moved to Berlin, and for the rest of his career supervised the king's private concerts, writing new works for them (including some of his six hundred sonatas and concertos for flute), and exercising his exclusive right to criticize Frederick's playing. For new compositions and making flutes, he received additional payments. Quantz's *Versuch einer Anweisung die Flöte traversiere zu spielen* (1752), his wide-ranging treatise, remains his most significant musical legacy.

Considering that keyboard players had long been moving toward irregular temperaments where there was no differentiation between sharped and flatted notes like D♯ and E♭—enharmonics, as we call them—this is a remarkable demonstration that non-keyboard players—singers, string players, and wind players alike—continued to treat them as separate pitches.

CHAPTER FOUR

"How Long, O Lord, How Long?"

Also, it is important to recognize that such enharmonic modulations, where they are genuine, do really mystify the listener, whether the instrument is a rigidly tempered affair like the pianoforte with all its distinctions ironed out into twelve semitones to the octave, or whether, like the human voice, the violin, and the slide-trombone, it makes its own intonation and can approach mathematical ideals to the limits of human muscular accuracy.

DONALD FRANCIS TOVEY, *Beethoven* (ca.1936)[1]

ONE MIGHT THINK, having passed the middle of the eighteenth century, that this kind of tuning system would inexorably and inevitably give way to ET. Surely Mozart in his maturity, out from under his father's thumb, would see the light.

Actually Leopold wrote to Wolfgang on June 11, 1778, and mentioned Tosi as an authority on tuning, but Wolfgang did not reply since his mother had passed away, and he had to send that sad news to his father. That understandable but unfortunate silence notwithstanding, and setting aside whatever tuning system Mozart may have used on his fortepiano—very likely some kind of irregular temperament—we do have evidence that Wolfgang recognized the same kind of differentiated enharmonic notes described by his father and Tosi and the other writers mentioned above.

In the summer of 1785, a nineteen-year-old English music student, Thomas Attwood, arrived in Vienna and for a year and a half took composition lessons from Mozart. From this interaction several pages survive with exercises and annotations by both men. Since Attwood's German wasn't very good, Mozart wrote in Italian and Attwood in English. The descriptions of intervals in Attwood's pages include Mozart's handwritten indications of "*mezzo tuono grande*" (major semitone) and "*mezzo tuono piccolo*" (minor semitone), and it is absolutely clear that the diatonic semitone is large and the chromatic semitone is small.

Figure 11. Mozart's Major and Minor Semitones.

In the top line of this detail, you can see three diatonic semitones labeled "*mezzi tuoni grandi*" (large half tones); the second line, showing chromatic semitones, is labeled "*mezzi tuoni piccoli*" (small half tones); the third line labels three notes as "*unisono*," "*unisono superfluo*," and "*seconda min[ore]*"; the second and third notes (the chromatic and diatonic semitones) are described as intervals against the note in the fourth line as "*mezzo tuono piccolo*" and "*mezzo tuono grande.*"

Thomas Attwood

Thomas Attwood was baptized in London on November 23, 1765, and died there on March 24, 1838. His father, also named Thomas Attwood, was a household servant to King George III, as well as a viola player and trumpeter at court. At nine young Thomas became a choirboy in the Chapel Royal. After his voice

broke, he entered the service of the Prince of Wales, who was so impressed with his musicality that he sent him to the Continent to study. From 1783 to 1785 he studied in Naples, then traveled to Vienna, where he lived from August 1785 until February 1787, still apparently supported by the Prince of Wales, and taking composition lessons from Mozart. Mozart seems to have been very fond of his young student, at one point writing good-naturedly in

Thomas Attwood, lithograph by Waller, from Attwood's Cathedral Music *(1850?).*

Each tone is thus comprised of a major and a minor semitone, and as in Tosi's 55-division, Mozart describes the octave as consisting of "5 *tuoni, e 2 semitoni grandi.*" Attwood himself annotates the table of intervals that includes the enharmonic variations saying, "These tones the Harpsichord has not, but all other Instruments have." The inescapable conclusion is that Mozart differentiated keyboard and non-keyboard tuning, and

English when Attwood had misread the clefs of an assignment, "You are an ass." He is also reported to have said of him, "He partakes more of my style than any scholar I ever had, and I predict that he will prove a sound musician." Attwood later repaid the debt to his teacher by helping to introduce Mozart's music to British audiences.

In 1796 Attwood became organist of St. Paul's Cathedral and later composer to the Chapel Royal as well. During this same period he began a successful career as a composer for the stage: From about 1792 to 1802, he provided music for more than thirty productions. In 1813 he joined thirty associates in founding the Philharmonic Society, and conducted one of their concerts almost every year thereafter, usually including something by his late teacher. In 1821 he composed a coronation anthem for King George IV, his former patron, and later wrote coronation music for William IV and Victoria, as well. He was a founding professor of the Royal Academy of Music in 1823. In his later years, he enjoyed a close friendship with Mendelssohn, who was a frequent houseguest. Attwood seems to have been profoundly affected by his experience as a pupil of Mozart, and his compositions reflect that in their approach to both melody and harmony. His grave lies beneath the organ in St. Paul's Cathedral.

---

regarded the standard non-keyboard tuning to include higher flatted notes and lower sharped notes.

I'm going to step aside from the historical narrative here to deal with an aspect of modern performance that frequently arises in the music of Mozart. Among modern musicians the ones who are perhaps more sensitive to tuning adjustments than any others are string chamber players. Most of them recognize that ET fifths

Mozart at the Interval Café drive-thru

HOW EQUAL TEMPERAMENT RUINED HARMONY

are not quite pure, and that pure major thirds are much, much narrower than in ET. Many further understand that the high leading-note, "expressive" tuning approach has its problems. As Arnold Steinhardt, first violinist of the renowned Guarneri Quartet says:

> The difficulty in string-quartet intonation is to determine the degree of freedom you have at any given moment. Two factors come into play: the linear and the vertical. By "linear" I'm referring to the sense of melodic or harmonic direction in the individual line; semitones in particular have a tendency to be drawn slightly up or down as the case may be. In this sense, "expressive intonation" is an essential element of interpretation. The other factor— the vertical—is the necessity to be in tune with your colleagues, to hear your individual note in relation to the chord being played at that moment. Both factors are important and demand a highly responsive ear and instant adaptability.
>
> Among the "vertical" considerations there are anchor points: these are octaves, fourths, and fifths. When played simultaneously these intervals should be exact [i.e., played with pure (or just) rather than equal-tempered intonation]. I make mental notes as to where they occur. I'll know that in bar 9 of a certain movement I play a B above the viola's F sharp, and this therefore leaves me virtually no leeway for subjectivity in intonation. I say "virtually" because every rule can have an exception: a problem may arise, for instance, if I want my B to lead to a C that follows. Should I play the B high? That's a hard choice to make and shows how the linear and vertical demands sometimes conflict.
>
> Arnold Steinhardt, quoted in *The Art of Quartet Playing: The Guarneri Quartet in Conversation with David Blum* (1986)[2]

The consensus nowadays seems to be that intonation in the finest string quartets and other unaccompanied chamber ensembles aspires to Just intonation, where fifths and fourths and thirds are all pure. Actually Steinhardt seems to be describing a practical compromise, where prominent fifths and fourths are all pure, and thirds are "improved" over their ET or "expressive" placement or perhaps made pure in certain circumstances. Even musicologists have tried to make a case for Just intonation as an historical practice for strings: one eminent twentieth-century scholar published an article arguing that Just intonation was what Prelleur and his eighteenth-century colleagues had in mind with the differentiated accidentals on his fingerboard diagram.[3] Just intonation actually shares with the extended meantone system I have been describing a differentiation of the accidentals by one comma, just as Leopold Mozart, Quantz, and Tosi recommended. So why do I *not* think these writers are referring to Just intonation? And why should modern players consider the extended meantone system, rather than Just intonation, as an alternative to ET? Shouldn't a system in which everything is pure be the ideal?

For many years I have been an outspoken advocate of Just intonation in the performance of early—mainly Renaissance—vocal ensemble works,[4] but beginning with the Baroque era, I don't think it works well, and I don't think it's what the composers had in mind for their own music, except, perhaps, for passages of unusually stable harmony. For one thing Just intonation, systematically applied, requires not only the differentiation of the accidentals but also two different sizes of whole tone. I think that's altogether too much flexibility to be usable for most music and instruments of the time. Though string players could probably manage it through the alternative use of open and stopped strings, woodwind players would find it impossible to adjust the "white notes" of their scales to the extent necessary to make different-size whole tones and, of course, keyboard instruments would be at a complete loss as well. Besides, neither wind instrument fingering charts nor keyboard tuning directions of the

Baroque and Classical periods suggest that Just intonation was what they were trying to achieve.

The real "clincher" as far as I am concerned, however, is the 55-division concept. Tosi and other writers say that the major semitone is five commas and the minor semitone is four commas. That one-comma differentiation is the part that Just intonation shares. But what Just intonation does not share is a universally usable nine-comma whole tone. One of Just intonation's two sizes of whole tone has nine commas (with a slightly larger comma), but two of them together create a major third that is much too wide to be acceptable—in fact, it's the Pythagorean major third (or ditone), mentioned by Benade, which is much wider even than ET. Thus if the whole tone can be described as being a single size, and that single size works in a consistent system with the differentiated semitones, then that eliminates Just intonation as the tuning system musicians of the time had in mind.

So while I can't argue with string quartet players for wanting to play pure intervals whenever they have the time and opportunity to use them in their performances, I think they should be adapting from extended meantone rather than ET. In fact, if you are already differentiating the semitones by a comma in your normal playing, it's easier to move momentarily to a chord that incorporates a pure interval against the already raised or lowered note.

I would actually question, moreover, whether it serves the music well to tune absolutely pure *thirds* except perhaps at movement endings and other places of arrival and repose. And perhaps I should also question whether modern quartet performers are really tuning pure thirds or, in consciously going against the high leading notes of "expressive intonation," they are simply tuning thirds that are *somewhat* narrower than those in ET—like those in extended sixth-comma meantone, for example, which as I mentioned, are almost exactly halfway between ET and pure. The acoustically pure major third is so far out of the normal scale that it could wreak havoc with the linear aspect of a phrase. Using pure major thirds also compromises the tuning in more complex harmonies. For example, an E that is lowered to be a pure major third above C would sound fine in a C-major triad, but it damages the quality of the tritone or diminished fifth against the B♭ in a C dominant-seventh chord.

One of the most significant features of extended sixth-comma meantone is that *all* the tritones and diminished fifths are acoustically pure.* So, as a player, you have to ask yourself, "What's more important to making this music go? Stability of triads, or dynamism of complex harmonies?" In most music after 1600, I would argue that the complex harmonies win out, and that means that extended meantone, not Just intonation, is the ideal. Of course, modern players will also ask themselves whether the horizontal or vertical aspects of the music are more important. Too often, I would say, musicians today choose to favor the horizontal, but that may not always be best for the music, and it is certainly not what any Baroque or Classical composers were thinking.

---

*Curiously, in his *Critica Musica* II of 1725, Johann Mattheson referred to Gottfried Silbermann's temperament (which we know to have been sixth-comma meantone in 1714) as "pure" (*rein*) compared with circulating temperaments (see pp. 237–38). This is an interesting usage and reflects the same kind of view as do Leopold Mozart's and Quantz's terms "proper" and "true." Certainly, by the end of the eighteenth century, writers like Galeazzi (mentioned below) are using "pure" to describe Just intonation, on which, see below. As late as the mid-eighteenth century, however, Telemann was describing his own system (which we know to have been extended sixth-comma meantone) as "pure, or nearly so" (*wo nicht völlig, doch bey nahe, rein*). See his *Neues musicalisches System* (1742–43) published in Lorenz C. Mizler, *Neu eröffnete musikalische Bibliothek* 3/4 (1752/R 1966), 713–19.

HOW EQUAL TEMPERAMENT RUINED HARMONY

For example, Arnold Steinhardt cites the following passage from Mozart's G minor Quintet (K. 516):

Ex. 1. W. A. Mozart: Quintet in G Minor (K. 516), first mvt., allegro, *mm. 92–94.*

Of the notes in the first violin part, Steinhardt says, "The F sharp in bar 93 should be drawn ever so slightly higher than the G flat in the previous bar."[5] That comment certainly reflects the common wisdom of modern "expressive intonation" practice, but it should be clear by now that it's exactly the opposite of what Mozart would have expected. Does that matter? Are modern practices better than what Mozart had in mind? I don't think so, and I don't think most musicians would deliberately go against the expectations of a composer like Mozart if they knew what those expectations were. And even though the sound of lower sharps and higher flats is likely to be unfamiliar to many musicians, I think Mozart's endorsement makes it worth trying . . . and trying very seriously.

Another aspect of the extended meantone system that frequently gets ignored is the beauty and interest of the unequal semitones, something which becomes very obvious in highly chromatic passages like the following from the last movement of Mozart's G Major Quartet (K. 387):

Ex. 2. W. A. Mozart: Quartet in G Major (K. 387), last mvt., molto allegro, mm. 123–31.

Of this passage, Guarneri Quartet violist Michael Tree says:

We would raise the sharpened notes slightly, but in this case we have to be a little careful because the motif is repeated many times, and if the intonation is exaggerated it may tend to sound increasingly so with the repetitions. We definitely believe in expressive intonation, but it has to be treated with care. We've heard playbacks of our performances that have alerted us to the danger of going too far. However, I'd sooner err in that direction than play with a sterile and static equal-tempered intonation.

Michael Tree, quoted in The Art of Quartet Playing:
The Guarneri Quartet in Conversation
with David Blum (1986)[6]

I absolutely agree with Michael Tree that ET in this passage is "sterile and static," although I would probably have said "boring and aimless." The alternating major-minor-major-minor-major semitones in a passage like that—as Mozart would have expected for a succession of diatonic and chromatic semitones—are precisely what give it life and direction and even humor. And they do not result in a tendency to rise in pitch like the repeated use of "expressive" intonation—ever-ascending sharps. The extended meantone system simply requires that all the diatonic semitones (from one pitch name to another) are large, and all the chromatic semitones (within one pitch name) are small. That's consistent and easy to remember, and the musical result is varied and beautiful, even though it's bound to be unfamiliar to most modern musicians at first.

CHAPTER FIVE

A Bridge to the Nineteenth Century

> It is necessary that the three open string 5ths be a little narrow, and
> this is the way violin players tune them in practice, the majority of
> them without knowing why.
>
> LUIGI PICCHIANTI, Principi Generali e Ragionati
della Musica Teorico-Pratica (1834)[1]

A FEW YEARS AFTER Mozart's instructions for Thomas
Attwood, we find a prominent German musical theorist, Daniel
Gottlob Türk, echoing the same approach to tones and semi-
tones:

> Each tone consists of two semitones, of which one is large and the
> other small. In order to comprehend this, it must be understood
> that a whole tone (c–d), i.e., the distance from c to d, usually con-
> sists of nine parts (commas), or in other words, that d is higher than
> c by nine commas; further, that a large semitone, i.e., d–e-flat, con-
> sists of five such parts, but the small semitone (e-flat to e) only of
> four, or four commas from d to d♯ and five from d♯ to e.
>
> Daniel Gottlob Türk, Klavierschule (1789)[2]

Türk was a keyboard player writing for keyboard players, but
he didn't shrink from "telling it like it is":

Daniel Gottlob Türk

Daniel Gottlob Türk, German theorist and composer, was born at Claussnitz on August 10, 1750, and died at Halle on August 26, 1813. His father, Daniel, was an instrumentalist in the service of Count Schönburg. The boy was first taught music by his father and studied various wind instruments with his father's colleagues. At the Dresden Kreuzschule he received a rigorous musical education before entering the University of Leipzig in 1772. In 1774 he

Daniel Gottlob Türk, from a contemporary engraving in the Bärenreiter-Archiv (Kassel).

became *Kantor* at the Ulrichskirche in Halle, which was then to remain his place of residence until his death. After 1776 his compositional activities focused mainly on keyboard music.

In 1779 Türk became director of music at Halle University, teaching theory and composition and, later, music history. In 1787 an appointment at the Marktkirche, Halle's principal church, enabled him to relinquish his post at the Gymnasium and focus on his musical work. In 1789 his *Klavierschule* appeared. Around 1799 Türk was working on a *Violinschule*, which was never completed or, at least, never published. His last theoretical work was the comprehensive temperament treatise, *Anleitung zu Temperaturberechnungen* (1808). His later years were enlivened by his work with his most famous pupil, the *Lieder* composer Carl Loewe. Türk was a man of exceptional learning, and clearly enjoyed the respect of his contemporaries.

The fact that these sizes of tones do not occur on the keyboard in their true proportions is due to the instrument's imperfection . . . and does not prove anything contrary to the actual differences of these tones. These tones can and should be produced on the violin, flute, oboe, and many other instruments, as well as in singing, as far as their higher or lower differentiation is concerned, according to their mathematical proportions.

Daniel Gottlob Türk, Klavierschule (1789)[3]

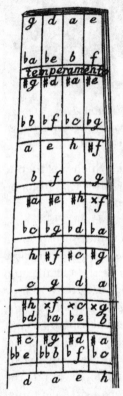

After Mozart's death, we find the first isolated references to the "higher leading note" practice. One that has been cited is that of Francesco Galeazzi in vol. 2 of his *Elementi Teorico-Pratici di Musica* (1796). In fact Galeazzi's comment on raising the leading note "to fully satisfy the ear" comes after twenty pages of discussion of Just intonation, where the leading note is very low as a pure major third above the fifth. It would be hard to interpret that as calling for leading notes that are higher than ET. On the other hand Campagnoli's *Nuovo Metodo della Mecanica Progressiva* (1797?)* really does call for notes to be differentiated, with the sharps higher than the flats. This can be seen in his fingerboard diagram (figure 12), showing the opposite note placement to Prelleur's.

Figure 12. Fingerboard Diagram. Bartolomeo Campagnoli,
Nuovo Metodo della Mecanica Progressiva (1797?), p. 129.

*Although Campagnoli's treatise is usually ascribed to the year 1797, no copies of that original edition survive, and it's unclear whether it did, in fact, appear that early. The first surviving version is a parallel Italian/French edition, printed in Florence sometime between 1808 and 1815.

HOW EQUAL TEMPERAMENT RUINED HARMONY

Many people think that, from this point on, this new linear approach became the standard at the same time that ET was becoming the dominant keyboard temperament. It was a long time before anyone else agreed with Campagnoli in print, however; and meanwhile there is plenty of evidence that the older, harmonic practice continued—at least as a parallel tradition.

On the cusp of the nineteenth century it was still going strong. Violinist Michel Woldemar, in his *Grande Méthode* (Paris, 1798–99/1802–03), gives a chromatic scale (figure 13) that includes both D♯ and E♭, G♯ and A♭, and even C♯ and D♭ at the upper end:

Figure 13. Chromatic scale from Michel Woldemar, Grande Méthode *(1798–99/1802–03), p. 3.*

Woldemar says:

> The chromatic scale is notated thus to show that on string instruments there is still a comma (the ninth part of a tone) difference between D♯ and E♭ and between G♯ and A♭—a difference that is not appreciated on wind instruments or on the piano.
>
> Michel Woldemar, *Grande Méthode* (1798–99)[4]

Woldemar exempts the winds in addition to the piano, but the message is the same. The standard practice among string players was to differentiate enharmonic notes by a comma. And Woldemar's whole tone is nine times that discrepancy.

Between the first and second editions of Woldemar's *Méthode*, Haydn was in Vienna writing his last complete string quartet: Op. 77, no. 2 in F, which he finished in 1799 and published in 1802. The autograph score—that is, a score in Haydn's own handwriting—

Bartolomeo Campagnoli

Bartolomeo Campagnoli was born at Cento, near Bologna, on September 10, 1751, and died at Neustrelitz, near Berlin, on November 7, 1827. After early studies in Bologna and Modena, he returned home in 1766 to play in a local orchestra. Then, after periods of further study in Venice and Padua, he settled in Florence, where he studied under Nardini and served as leader of the second violins at the Teatro della Pergola. He went to Rome in 1775 to fill the same post at the Teatro Argentina, but after a year he left Italy and entered the service of the bishop of Freysingen. For most of 1778 he seems to have toured extensively in northern Europe. That must have been highly successful because in Stockholm he was elected a member of the Swedish Royal Academy of Music. In 1779 he became director of music at the Duke of Courland's court in Dresden, but continued concertizing all over Europe.

After the death of the duke of Courland, Campagnoli became leader of the Leipzig Gewandhaus Orchestra in 1797, and his touring essentially ceased. He visited Paris in 1801, however, where he was greatly impressed with the playing of Rodolphe Kreutzer. In 1816 he toured with his two daughters, both of whom

survives and contains some striking and highly unusual markings related to tuning. In the development section of the first movement, in the cello part, he writes *"l'istesso tuono"* between an E♭ and a D♯ (see figure 14). At the same time he indicates a change of finger from the middle to the index finger of the cellist's left hand and also specifies *"das leere A"* in the first violin, meaning that the first violinist should play the note A on the open second

Violinist (Campagnoli?), from the Florentine edition of his treatise (1815?).

were singers, to Italy, Frankfurt, Hannover, and finally, in 1826, to Neustrelitz, where he himself may have held a position for the year before his death.

Spohr reported that Campagnoli's playing was clean and fluent but his method antiquated. Indeed, in his *Nouvelle Méthode*, Campagnoli's manner of holding the bow is conservative, although, on the subject of tuning, he seems to have been an innovator even if his treatise was not published as early as 1797, as once thought. However, its logical order and carefully graded exercises found many admirers. An English edition was published in 1856 in London and later in Boston.

string of the instrument instead of stopping the D string. What does all this mean?

It's not entirely clear, but I have a theory. First of all Haydn's stipulation that E♭ and D♯ should be *"l'istesso tuono"*—"the same note"—in itself confirms that he expected the player would normally play them as differentiated pitches. In ET, of course, they are the same note, so it's only in a system like extended mean-

Figure 14. Josef Haydn, Quartet op. 77, no. 2 (autograph, 1799), first mvt.

tone, where they are *different*, that a special indication like this would be required. Since Haydn is about to use what's called an "enharmonic modulation"—in this case, changing keys by treating the E♭ as if it were really a D♯—he calls for the pitch to stay the same (in spite of the expected change of finger) in order to enhance the surprise, as it were. That, at any rate, is my explanation of why he did it. The open string A in the first violin then makes a tritone against the E♭ whereas it would have made a diminished fifth against the D♯. Both are pure in extended sixth-comma meantone, but it takes a precise placement of the A in order to get the most out of the pure interval, and calling for an open string achieves that by removing the possibility of vibrato. It is quite possible, even likely, in my opinion, that Haydn expected the cellist eventually to change the pitch of the D♯ to an actual D♯ from that of the slightly higher E♭, since the note then alternates with the E natural above it, and it would be easy to lower the D♯

HOW EQUAL TEMPERAMENT RUINED HARMONY

Michel Woldemar

Michel Woldemar, violinist and composer, was baptized at Orléans on September 21, 1750, and died at Clermont-Ferrand on December 19, 1815. Born into a wealthy family, he took his name from his godfather Woldemar, count of Lowendal, marshal of France. According to Orléans historian Denis Lottin, in his youth Michel was held prisoner at the Sabot d'Angers, where he developed his talent for the violin. In Paris, he studied with Antonio Lolli and became accomplished enough to tour. By his own report, about 1770 in Madrid, he performed his "Fandango, air favori des Espagnols"—later published in his *Six Rêves d'un Violon Seul* (1803)—and he took part in the famous salon concerts sponsored by the wealthy Parisian patron, Baron Charles Ernest de Bagge.

A "reversal of fortune" (the French Revolution, perhaps?) compelled him to earn his living by playing, and he left Orléans and toured with a troupe of traveling comedians. In June 1801, however, he owned a vineyard in Orléans. By April 1804 he had moved to Paris, where he gave lessons and worked as an accompanist. Finally, in about 1807 he settled in Clermont-Ferrand, where he taught at the cathedral choir school.

Anticipating the modern jazz vogue for five-string electric violins, around 1788, Woldemar championed and wrote for an acoustic version of such an instrument, which he called the "violon-alto." It had a lower C string, giving it the range of the violin and viola combined.

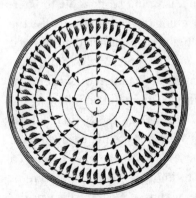

Woldemar's Chart of Note Values from his Méthode d'Alto *(ca. 1800–1805); engraved by Van-ixem.*

once that alternation begins. And Haydn's marking may in fact refer specifically to the first D♯, since he carefully drew vertical lines beneath the last E♭ and the first D♯.

The special tuning indication was transferred from Haydn's autograph to his copyist's parts and into the first printed edition in 1802 (figure 15).

Figure 15. Josef Haydn, Quartet op. 77, no. 2 (first edition, 1802), cello part, first mvt.

But as ET gradually became the "standard" tuning system in the nineteenth century, calling D♯ and E♭ the same note must have seemed more and more superfluous. Of *course* it was the same note! Thus the marking was omitted from later editions, and the evidence that Haydn expected an *unequal* tuning system was expunged from the record.

Now, in fairness to Campagnoli, it would be possible to interpret Haydn's *"l'istesso tuono"* as warning the cellist not to raise the D♯, according to the new linear preference, rather than lower it according to the older harmonic practice. I personally think, however, that the strength of the harmonic tradition was such that Haydn could not have *assumed* his players would be following the newer style. Besides, he was sixty-eight years old by then, and as we all know the musical habits of a lifetime are not easily broken.

A decade earlier, moreover, Haydn is known to have admired a complicated keyboard designed to improve the "temperature of the thirds and fifths" and do away with the "wolfe." This was the Telio-chordon, a kind of fortepiano patented by Londoner Charles Claggett in 1788, where each octave was divided into thirty-nine notes, accessed by means of pedals. Haydn wrote to

Claggett in April 1792: "Sir! I called at your house, during your absence, and examined your improvements on the Pianoforte, and Harpsichords, and I found you had made them perfect instruments. I therefore, in justice to your invention, cannot forbear giving you my full approbation, as by this means you have rendered one of the finest instruments ever invented, perfect, and therefore the fittest to conduct any musical performance, and to accompany the human voice."[5] This kind of enthusiasm for an intonation device of such subtle variety—thirty-nine notes to the octave—argues against any inclination toward ET on Haydn's part.

The same year that Haydn's last quartet was published, 1802, Beethoven set down, in his so-called Heiligenstadt Testament, an account of how he himself was growing inexorably and irreversibly deaf. Whatever the movement of the musical world toward ET during the following decades, it's difficult to see how Beethoven, in his deafness, could have "evolved" away from the standard tuning of his first thirty years toward a new arrangement of tones and semitones. One of the few clues to Beethoven's tuning expectations comes from the composer's biographer and self-described amanuensis, Anton Felix Schindler. In response to the discussion of key characteristics in Christian Friedrich Daniel Schubart's *Ideen zu einer Aesthetik der Tonkunst* (1806), of which Beethoven reportedly owned a copy, Schindler reports:

> As for instrumental music, especially quartets and orchestral works, Beethoven generally disregarded Schubart's characterization of the keys because many of them were ambiguous or impracticable. He did, however, accept them up to a point in his piano solos and trios.
>
> Anton Felix Schindler, *Biographie von Ludwig van Beethoven* (1860)[6]

This is an interesting observation. Why would Beethoven concede the validity of key characteristics in piano music but not in quartets, for example? The obvious answer, in my opinion, is that Beethoven thought in terms of some kind of irregular temperament for his piano, where the "personalities" of the keys are heightened by myriad differences in scales and harmonies in each key. Well into the nineteenth century, writers commented on this issue and came to the same conclusion about ET and key characteristics:[7]

> An equal temperament, however, cannot subsist, or else we would no longer have any key characteristics, and one could just as well compose a nocturne in A minor, and a military blare in A♭ major.
>
> Pietro Lichtenthal, *Dizionario e Bibliografia della Musica* (1826)[8]

> The opinion has been very generally entertained among musicians that there is a peculiar character belonging to each of the keys. We should not have considered this opinion worthy of notice in this connection, but for the reason that many have attributed this real, or supposed, peculiar character to temperament. . . . If an instrument be tuned in the *equal temperament*—which is the more common and popular—every key is tempered *precisely alike*, and consequently all peculiarity from the cause assigned will disappear.
>
> H. W. Poole, "An Essay on Perfect Musical Intonation in the Organ" (1850)[9]

> If an instrument of fixed tones is completely and uniformly tuned according to the equal temperament, so that all Semitones throughout the scale have precisely the same magnitude, and if also the musical quality of all the tones is precisely the same, there seems to be no ground for understanding how each different key should have a different character.
>
> Hermann von Helmholtz, *Die Lehre den Tonempfindungen als physiologische Grundlage für die Theorie der Musik* (1863)[10]

String instruments, of course, don't use temperament—or at least don't *have* to use temperament—they can place the notes

HOW EQUAL TEMPERAMENT RUINED HARMONY

where they want to and are not fixed like a piano. The two possibilities for the discrepancy in Beethoven's view of key characteristics, it seems to me, are that either he recognized that strings would be playing in ET and therefore that the really striking differences in the keys would be diminished, or he recognized that the strings would be playing in extended meantone, where the same thing would be true. Within each of these systems, every major or minor scale is identical to every other major or minor scale in terms of interval size, and thus the chords and melodic characteristics of the different keys would not be as individualized as they would be in an irregular keyboard temperament. But ET is not really a possibility. Given the history of string playing through Beethoven's hearing years, and the similarity of the quality of the consonances between extended meantone and irregular keyboard temperaments, I think it virtually certain that Beethoven was recognizing that the strings would be placing the notes in their traditional "true" positions, according to the extended meantone system. This is in spite of the fact that his quartets, for example, contain about a half dozen instances of enharmonic modulation like that in Haydn's op. 77, no. 2, where some kind of compromise pitch would be required, at least momentarily.

By 1818 Beethoven was virtually stone deaf, but I think it's fair to say that everyone today, including players involved in the historical performance movement, generally believes that by that time ET was the dominant, if not exclusive, tuning system in ensemble music as well as piano music, and that variants from ET—if they existed—were toward the high leading note practice. But in that year, the French theorist Pierre Galin published his *Rationale for a New Way of Teaching Music*, describing a tuning system in which the whole tones are all the same size and each is made up of one major and one minor semitone. Sound familiar?

Galin's "new way" eventually became the Galin-Paris-Chevé

Pierre Galin

Pierre Galin was born at Samatan, "the city of *foie gras*," near Toulouse, in 1786, and died at Bordeaux on August 31, 1821. He studied at the Lycée in Bordeaux and also spent time at the École Polytechnique there, working on mathematics, astronomy, physics, and political economics. He was first employed by a banker who noticed his remarkable aptitude for mathematics, discouraged his stated plan of emigrating to the United States, and urged him to go into teaching. Galin taught at the Lycée— his former school—and then at the Royal Institute for Deaf-Mutes. Having a talent for music, he next turned his attention to that, but decided that music teaching was ineffective because it attempted to combine elements of rhythm and melody in a confusing way, and failed to train the ear before introducing complex notational concepts. Based on his scientific analysis of music theory, Galin began to teach a group of children, and, after a year with some success, published an account of his method in *Exposition d'une Nouvelle Méthode pour l'Enseignement de la Musique* (Paris, 1818), later translated into English as *Rationale for a New Way of Teaching Music* (Kilkenny, Ireland, 1983). The book was a revolutionary analysis of the problems of teaching music, and its success prompted Galin to take his ideas to Paris in 1819. He taught classes of children but also trained a number of teachers in his method, before dying in 1821 at the age of thirty-five, reportedly from a chest ailment brought on by overwork. Although several of his pupils, including Philippe

Pierre Galin teaching from Exposition d'une Nouvelle Méthode *(1818).*

Geslin, attempted to continue Galin's work, Aimé Paris had the most success. Together with his sister Nanine and her husband, Émile Chevé, Paris developed Galin's simple approach into a full course of study with its own textbooks and exercises. It enjoyed wide international use and survives in some places even today.

Method, which achieved wide popularity among music educators all over Europe in the second half of the nineteenth century. In fact Galin himself died at the age of thirty-five in 1821, but his major and minor semitones were expounded by his disciple Philippe Marc Antoine Geslin in 1825, as follows:

> We have said, besides, that in practice, one acts as if the sharp and flat divide the natural major seconds equally. This is evident on fixed keyboard instruments, like the piano for example. The same black key serving to make A♭ or G♯, equally divides the interval of the major second, G to A. But the majority of musicians think that these two notes, A♭ and G♯, should not be rendered by the same key, and that if this is done for the convenience of instrument manufacture, the ear suffers for it and is forced to make concessions in order to hear the flats with the same system of keys that forms the sharps. One supposes generally, therefore, that the sharp and the flat unequally divide the major seconds. There are many different opinions on the proportion of this division; the most accredited is that the distance from a note to its sharp or its flat is smaller than what's left [of the major second]. Thus . . . the interval from F to F♯ is calculated to be smaller than that from F♯ to G. The interval from G to G♭ is calculated to be smaller than that from G♭ to F. If this happens, there is a small distance from F♯ to G♭, and instruments on which the same key renders both sounds are false. This distance . . . is called the *comma*.
>
> Philippe Marc Antoine Geslin, *Cours Analytiques de Musique,*
> *ou Méthode Développée du Méloplaste* (1825)[11]

In 1827, in "Numerical Values of the Notes of the Scale," another French theorist, Charles Édouard Joseph Delezenne, took exception to some details in the Galin/Geslin system. Galin considered the proportion between the major and minor semitone to be 3:2, rather than the 5:4 ratio of commas in the extended-sixth-comma meantone system I have been describing. The result is a kind of exaggeration of that system. Whereas

HOW EQUAL TEMPERAMENT RUINED HARMONY

Charles Delezenne

Charles Delezenne, son of a shopkeeper in Lille, near the Belgian border, was born on October 4, 1776, and died there on August 26, 1866. He showed promise as a science student and, along with other privileged students shortly after 1800, found himself in the same college class as Napoleon's wayward brother Jérôme. After teaching high school in Paris from 1803 to 1805, Delezenne returned to his native Lille as Professor of Mathematics, a post he held until his retirement in 1836. He also taught physics privately from 1817 to 1848. Although he was writing about music already in the 1820s, in his retirement Delezenne seems to have focused a great deal on acoustical issues, publishing *Expériences et Observations sur les Cordes des Instruments à Archet* (1853), *Considérations sur l'Acoustique Musicale* (1855), *Note sur le Ton des Orchestres et des Orgues* (1855?), and *Table de Logarithmes Acoustiques* (1857). He is reputed to have been the first to apply calculus to the solution of acoustics problems.

Charles Delezenne.
(Collection École Polytechnique, Lille)

extended sixth-comma meantone corresponds to the 55-division of the octave, Galin's system comes at it from the other direction: specifying that the major semitone should be 3/2 the minor semitone in effect creates a 31-note division of the octave (7 major + 5 minor semitones = (7 × 3) + (5 × 2) = 31 units) which, in turn, closely corresponds to extended-quarter-comma meantone, the classic Renaissance system with pure major thirds.[12] Although the interval size varies from the 55-division, the "shape" of the 31-division is the same, with lower sharps and higher flats.

Delezenne actually favors Just intonation and spends most of his treatise describing it (complete with pure major thirds and two different sizes of whole tone), but he does offer an "improved" version of the Galin/Geslin system as well. Curiously Delezenne's adjustment corresponds to extended fifth-comma meantone and the 43-division of the octave. Again the sharps are low and the flats are high, but his ratio of the major to minor semitone is 4:3, rather than 5:4 (as in Tosi) or 3:2 (as in Galin/Geslin). There aren't many other choices, as you can see,* but the melodic tendencies are all the same in these systems. The essential point is that both Galin/Geslin and Delezenne are describing systems with diatonic major and chromatic minor semitones, having seven major and five minor semitones to the octave, just as we have documented from well back in the eighteenth century. He also offers this comment on orchestral tuning:

> In a theater orchestra where the wind instruments mix with bowed strings, sharped notes are confused with the flatted notes

---

*The one important superparticular ratio missing from this list is 2:1, which gives a whole tone of three very large commas, with the major semitone twice the size of the minor semitone. This results in a 19-division of the octave and was recommended by Francisco de Salinas in the sixteenth century. One other important major/minor semitone ratio is 5:3, which results in a 50 division of the octave like that of Robert Smith's "equal harmony": 7 major + 5 minor semitones = (7 × 5) + (5 × 3) = 50 units.

above them, and even if one is able to differentiate notes through alternative fingerings or manipulation of the embouchure, they are never perfectly in tune, especially in keys other than those in which the instrument is centered. Bowed strings are forced to imitate these alterations, this temperament, and the result is that pieces written in certain passages and keys with lots of sharps and flats, take on a pallor, a somber tint at odds with the dramatic effect envisioned by the composer.

Charles Édouard Joseph Delezenne, "Sur les Valeurs
Numériques des Notes de la Gamme" (1826–27)[13]

Delezenne is obviously not happy with the tuning compatibility of wind and string instruments, but he clearly describes a situation where professional orchestral musicians are consciously attempting to differentiate their sharps and flats using the established harmonic approach of lower sharps and higher flats. Strings may have to place the notes in a compromise position when they play with instruments that are more limited in their ability to adjust, but the ideal is clearly the traditional harmonic approach. Delezenne is aware of ET, however, and has this comment about it:

[Equal] temperament is nevertheless the best that could be adopted for an instrument that confuses sharps and flats, and on which one wishes to play in all keys and modes in use.

Charles Édouard Joseph Delezenne, "Sur les Valeurs
Numériques des Notes de la Gamme" (1826–27)[14]

That it "confuses sharps and flats" is hardly a ringing endorsement of the new "standard."

CHAPTER SIX

Really Better or Simply Easier?

*The writer of this paper is of the opinion that . . . the same sound
can no more correctly represent C♯ and D♭, than the number 62 can
correctly represent the two products of 6 into 10, and 8 into 8.*

H. W. POOLE, "An Essay on Perfect Musical
Intonation in the Organ" (1850)[1]

I COULD HARDLY ARGUE that ET was not being used or
advocated by the second quarter of the nineteenth century. Still,
there's an unsettling sense that not everything is being said, and
that the situation may be more complicated than the writers are
letting on. One of the most influential string theorists of this
period was Louis Spohr, whose *Violinschule* (1832) was translated
into several languages and published as far away as America. Here,
from the preface, is Spohr's comment on intonation:

> Extreme patience and perseverance must be devoted to the 4th
> section [of the treatise], which lays the foundations of pure into-
> nation for the student. The teacher can indeed save himself great
> trouble in the future if he insists with uncompromising strictness
> right from the outset on the absolutely pure intonation of the
> pupil's stopped notes.
>
> Louis Spohr, *Violinschule* (1832)[2]

In a footnote, Spohr explains his terminology:

> By pure intonation is naturally meant that of equal temperament
> [*gleichschwebenden*], since in modern music no other exists.
>
> Louis Spohr, Violinschule (1832)[3]

Spohr does not leave much room for misintepretation: The only
tuning system that exists is ET! What could be clearer or more
direct? Why would I even bother to include a quote like that in a
book in which I am trying to argue against the exclusive use of ET?

The problem with Spohr's seemingly unequivocal endorsement of ET is that, even as it tries to reinforce the point, the continuation of this same footnote raises questions:

> The budding violinist needs to know only this one intonation. For
> this reason neither unequal temperament nor small and large
> semitones are mentioned in this method because both would
> serve only to confuse the doctrine of absolutely equal sizes of all
> 12 semitones.
>
> Louis Spohr, Violinschule (1832)[4]

This reminds me of the proscriptions against the use of musical instruments in churches during the Middle Ages. One church
father after another says, "No instruments are allowed in
church"; "Under no circumstances will instruments be allowed in
church"; "Instrumentalists are advised that they are forbidden to
bring their instruments into the church." If it wasn't already happening over and over again, why would all these reiterations of
the policy be necessary?

On the surface, Spohr seems to be saying that ET is the one
and only system. However, a closer reading reveals, first of all,
acknowledgment of the *existence* of both unequal temperaments
and major and minor semitones, and, second, a hint that he is
recommending ET because it's less confusing for the inexperi-
enced player. One perfectly logical interpretation of this passage

Louis Spohr

Louis Spohr was born in Brunswick in 1784 and died at Kassel in 1859. The son of a physician, he was christened Ludewig, but was always known as Louis. His mother was a gifted singer and pianist, his father a flute player, so early signs of Louis's musical talent were not surprising. He was given his first violin in 1789, and he studied locally before moving to Brunswick for further training. In the autumn of 1804, Spohr embarked on a successful concert tour, for which he

Louis Spohr, self-portrait. (Copyright Lebrecht Music & Arts.)

composed two concertos. By 1805, though only twenty-one, he was appointed *Konzertmeister* in Gotha.

Remaining there until 1812, Spohr grew more expert as a conductor and tried his hand at various compositional forms. He

would be that professional violinists in 1832 were using an *unequal* system but that Spohr thought it was simply too complicated for beginners.

In France around the same time, the most prominent writer on violin playing was François-Antoine Habeneck, former student of Pierre Baillot at the Paris Conservatoire and, from 1817, concertmaster and ultimately director of the Paris Opéra. His *Méthode Théorique et Pratique de Violon* appeared around 1835. In discussing intervals early in the book, Habeneck says:

also began to achieve recognition as an excellent teacher, eventually training many fine young violinists.

While touring in 1812–13 he agreed to become director of the orchestra of the Theater an der Wien in Vienna. He composed assiduously during his time there and made friends with Beethoven. In February 1815, however, he left Vienna for touring and concertizing in Switzerland, Italy, and Germany. Then, from late 1817 to 1819, he was director of opera in Frankfurt.

In October 1821 Spohr moved to Dresden, where he renewed his friendship with the composer Carl Maria von Weber. Through Weber he became *Kapellmeister* in Kassel, where he was to remain the rest of his life, primarily as the director of opera. The political disturbances of 1830 resulted in the closure of the opera during 1832–33, and Spohr's melancholy about the political situation discouraged him from even attempting opera for several years. It was then that he wrote his *Violinschule*, which became one of the best known and most admired violin methods of the century. Spohr's services as a conductor were often in demand during the years following, and indeed he remained active as a conductor until the final months of his life.

The augmented second and the minor third are, in effect, the same, but their designation changes with the names of the notes. For example, *G-natural* to $A\sharp$ forms an augmented second; with $B\flat$ one would have a minor third which, as noted, is formed from three semitones just like the augmented second. It's the same with regard to the augmented fourth and diminished fifth, the augmented fifth and minor sixth, and the augmented sixth and minor seventh. We do not seek here to establish the difference that actu-

Really Better or Simply Easier?

Spohr teaching all about tuning

HOW EQUAL TEMPERAMENT RUINED HARMONY

ally exists between these intervals, the study of which belongs more to composition.

François-Antoine Habeneck, *Méthode Théorique et Pratique de Violon* (ca.1835)[5]

The "difference that actually [*réellement*] exists" is an interesting phrase and again seems to acknowledge that enharmonic notes are not the same. This impression is strengthened later in the book where, after giving six pairs of enharmonically equivalent scales, he says:

> The intonation of the two scales joined by a bracket { is the same for instruments with predetermined or fixed notes such as the piano or organ; but it is perceptibly different on the violin or the bass which, since they are obliged to form their own notes, can modify infinitely the relationships between them.
>
> It is not part of the intention of this work to expatiate on the nature and extent of this difference, particularly since there is no need to take it into account except when the entire harmonic ensemble is produced by instruments with variable notes and one single instrument with fixed notes joins in, whereupon the main object must be to remove the difference forthwith if the intonation is not to be made intolerable; suffice it to say that this is done to prevent students being taken by surprise, which would plunge them into a state of distress and perplexity by making them doubt the accuracy of their own ears.

François-Antoine Habeneck, *Méthode Théorique et Pratique de Violon* (ca. 1835)[6]

Habeneck states, first of all, that nonfixed instruments can "modify infinitely" the relationships between the notes of the scale and implies that they do so whenever they are not encumbered by having to perform with a fixed-pitch instrument like the piano or organ. In that case they have to conform to what the fixed-pitch instrument is doing in order to avoid "intolerable" intonation. Like Spohr, Habeneck is reluctant to discuss the

François-Antoine Habeneck

François-Antoine Habeneck, the French violinist, conductor and composer, was born at Mézières on January 22, 1781, and died in Paris on February 8, 1849. He was a son of a Mannheim musician serving in the French army. Along with his two younger brothers, François-Antoine first studied violin with his father, then with Baillot at the Paris Conservatoire, where he won a *premier prix* in 1804, impressing the Empress Josephine with his artistry. That

same year, he joined the orchestra of the Opéra-Comique, then that of the Opéra. When, in 1817, Rodolphe Kreutzer was appointed to direct the Opéra, Habeneck succeeded him as principal violin. From 1821 until basically 1846, he was director of the Paris Opéra during one of its most celebrated eras, leading first performances of Rossini, Meyerbeer, and Berlioz, among others.

Habeneck taught the violin at the Conservatoire from 1808 to 1816 and from 1825 to 1848.

François-Antoine Habeneck. (Copyright Lebrecht Music & Arts)

His *Méthode Théorique et Pratique de Violon* appeared in about 1835. He is also credited with the introduction of Beethoven's music to France, leading performances of his symphonies as early as 1807. In 1828 the student orchestra he directed at the Conservatoire was regularized into a formal organization, the Société des Concerts du Conservatoire. Habeneck directed this large orchestra and chorus virtually every Sunday afternoon from November to April until his death, and tickets were so coveted that they were passed from generation to generation, like those of beloved sports teams today. The Société continued until 1967, when it was succeeded by the Orchestre de Paris.

Habeneck normally used his bow to conduct while serving as concertmaster, and some critics complained that he also took snuff during performances. Wagner, whose music Habeneck programmed as early as 1839, admired his efficiency and control, and claimed to have finally understood Beethoven's Ninth Symphony after hearing it under his direction. Habeneck had an enormous influence on the Parisian musical scene, particularly after the establishment of the Société. He played a late Stradivarius violin (the "Habeneck"), which is now owned by the Royal Academy of Music in London.

differentiation of notes in order to avoid distressing students. ET thus appears as the sanctioned system by virtue of its simplicity, not because of its superiority to other systems and not because it's what professional players were using. And yet the simple message bequeathed to us from these treatises is that ET is the only system that exists. We, in effect, have been the heirs of this mid-nineteenth-century pedagogical impulse to spare students the subtleties of professional tuning practices. Unlike Galin/Geslin and Delezenne a few years earlier, Spohr and Habeneck do not say which way the sharps and flats vary from one another, but they do confirm that they vary. We can only conclude that in 1835, professional string players still differentiated sharps and flats unless they had to perform with a fixed-pitch instrument.

Just as an aside, Habeneck's colleague, the virtuoso cellist and theorist Bernhard Romberg (1767–1841), is sometimes cited as recommending high leading notes. His treatise was reportedly adopted by Cherubini for cellists at the Paris Conservatoire in about 1840. In fact the recommendation he gives there to raise the leading note is an elementary reminder to alter the lowered leading note of the minor scale (like G-natural to G-sharp in A minor), not a prescription to raise the leading note beyond its normal tuning.[7] Romberg also distinguishes between "chromatic semitone" and "minor second" (that is, diatonic semitone),[8] and comments on enharmonic notes as follows: "I must not forget to remark, that whenever enharmonic notes occur, where it is necessary to change from a flat to a sharp, or the reverse, it will always be more advisable to let the finger remain in its place, than to change it."[9] Just as Haydn anticipated in figure 14, a change of finger seems to imply that the enharmonic notes were normally different.

In any event, unlike Spohr, Habeneck nowhere implies that his fixed-pitch instrument was in ET—just that it was fixed and that the sharps and flats were in a shared position that was different from the "normal" placement of those notes.* That compromise could be ET, of course, but it could just as easily describe any circulating temperament. What evidence exists for what keyboards were doing toward the middle of the nineteenth century?

*At least one French musician had strong feelings about the sharps being higher than the flats: Hector Berlioz, in his *Grand Traité d'Instrumentation et d'Orchestration Modernes* (Paris, 1844), ridiculed the old-fashioned tuning of the concertina with lower sharps, and said it was contrary to modern practice. He did say, however, that such linear tuning was to be used by "solo instrumentalists and singers," that "orchestral players should normally do without it," and that "the great majority of musicians disregard it in harmonic textures." See *Grand Traité*, ed. Peter Bloom (Kassel, 2003), pp. 466–70, and *Berlioz's Orchestration Treatise: A Translation and Commentary*, by Hugh McDonald (Cambridge, 2002), pp. 306–10.

Really Better or Simply Easier?

CHAPTER SEVEN

Some Are More Equal than Others

Equal temperament has this great advantage over all others—its twelve keys can all be used, they are all tempered alike. The ear, too, is better satisfied when all the chords are equally out of tune. [emphasis original]

H. W. POOLE, "An Essay on Perfect Musical Intonation in the Organ" (1850)[1]

ON SEPT. 1, 1811, in the *New Monthly Magazine,* James Broadwood of the famous Broadwood piano firm in London proposed the use of ET for pianos. Unfortunately his description of it there seems more like a kind of mild meantone—perhaps ninth comma—than ET per se. This was pointed out to him, and by November he "rejoined that he gave merely a practical method of producing equal temperament, 'from its being in most general use, and because of the various systems it has been pronounced the best deserving by Haydn, Mozart, and other masters of harmony.' Unfortunately, he gives no references, and consequently this assertion can be taken only as an unverified impression. . . ."[2] Indeed, the evidence suggests that it took much longer for ET to become anything like a standard, and "earwitness" accounts point to a time closer to the middle of the nineteenth century:

As regards Mr. James Broadwood's statement that equal temperament was in 1811 "in most general use" presumably in England—
Mr. Hipkins has been at some pains to ascertain how far that was
the case, and from him I learn that Mr. Peppercorn, who tuned originally for the Philharmonic Society, was concert tuner at Broadwoods', and a great favourite of Mr. James Broadwood. His son writes
to Mr. Hipkins that his father "always tuned so that all keys can be
played in, and neither he nor I [neither father nor son] ever held
with making some keys sweet and others sour." Mr. Bailey, however,
who succeeded Mr. Peppercorn as concert tuner, and tuned Mr.
James Broadwood's own piano at Lyne, his country house, used the
meantone temperament to Mr. Hipkins' own knowledge, and no
other. Not one of the old tuners Mr. Hipkins knew (and some had
been favourite tuners of Mr. James Broadwood) tuned anything like
equal temperament. Collard, the Wilkies, Challenger, Seymour, all
tuned the meantone temperament, except that, like Arnold Schlick,
1511, they raised the G♯ somewhat to mitigate the "wolf" resulting
from the Fifth E♭: G♯ in place of E♭: A♭. Hence, Mr. James Broadwood did not succeed in introducing equal temperament perma-
nently even into his own establishment, and all tradition of it died
out long ago. So far runs Mr. Hipkins' interesting information.

Alexander J. Ellis, "Additions by the Translator,"
in *On the Sensations of Tone* (1885)[3]

This interesting "inside" information comes from Alexander
Ellis, perhaps best known as an important historian of pitch, but
also as translator of Hermann von Helmholtz's seminal work on
musical acoustics, *Die Lehre von den Tonempfindungen als physiologische Grundlage für die Theorie der Musik* (1863). In addition to
translating what Helmholtz wrote, Ellis added a great deal by way
of commentary, and it is from those annotations that these comments are taken. Ellis goes on to give the following particulars:

It is one thing to propose equal temperament, to calculate its
ratios, and to have trial instruments approximately tuned in accor-

Hermann von Helmholtz

Hermann von Helmholtz, the great German scientist, was born in Potsdam on August 31, 1821, and died in Berlin on September 8, 1894. His father was a philosophy teacher, and his mother was a descendant of William Penn, the founder of Pennsylva-

nia. He received his doctorate in medicine at the Friedrich-Wilhelm Institut in Berlin in 1842, but his studies also included mathematics, physics, and philosophy (as well as piano on the side). Starting in 1848, after serving as an army surgeon, he held a series of professorships in medicine, beginning with Königsberg, then Bonn (1855), and Heidelberg (1858), and in physics at Berlin (1871). There, in 1887, he founded the Physikalisch-Technische Reichsanstalt, the first institute of pure scientific

Hermann von Helmholtz, ca. 1885. (Hulton Archive/ Getty Images)

dance with it, and another thing to use it commercially in all instruments sold. For pianos in England, it did not become a trade usage till 1846, at about which time it was introduced into Broadwoods' under the superintendence of Mr. Hipkins himself. At least eight more years elapsed before equal temperament was generally used for organs, on which its defects are more apparent, although not to such an extent as on the harmonium.

In 1851, at the Great Exhibition, no English organ was tuned in equal temperament, but the only German organ exhibited (Schulze's) was so tuned.

HOW EQUAL TEMPERAMENT RUINED HARMONY

research. His own research encompassed numerous aspects of human eye and ear physiology, optics, electrodynamics, mathematics, meteorology and, of course, acoustics. He is perhaps best known for his statement of the law of conservation of energy. He also invented the ophthalmoscope.

After becoming interested in acoustics around 1852, Helmholtz illuminated many areas of the subject, including the nature of beats and their role in consonance and dissonance, the role of harmonics in timbre, the nature of combination tones, and "summation tones" (equal to the combined frequencies of the two notes in an interval), which supported his theory of the nonlinearity of the ear (that is, that through interaction with aural stimuli, the ear was capable of providing sounds that were not specifically generated). His work on the ear led to the foundation of the resonance theory of hearing (that is, that tiny elements within the ear resonate sympathetically, like miniature piano strings, with incoming tones). In addition he studied phase in sound waves and invented a microscope to investigate wave patterns. Helmholtz, in short, was an intellectual giant who laid the foundations for modern acoustics.

In July 1852 Messrs. J. W. Walker & Sons put their Exeter Hall organ into equal temperament, but it was not used publicly till November of that year. Meanwhile, in Sept., Mr. George Herbert, a barrister and amateur, then in charge of the organ in the Roman Catholic Church in Farm St., Berkeley Square, London, had that organ tuned equally by Mr. Hill, the builder. Though much opposed, it was visited and approved by many, and among others by Mr. Cooper, who had the organ in the hall of Christ's Hospital (the Bluecoat School) tuned equally in 1853.

In 1854 the first organ built and tuned originally in equal temperament by Messrs. Gray & Davison was made for Dr. Fraser's Congregational Chapel at Blackburn (both chapel and organ have since been burned). In the same year Messrs. Walker and Mr. Willis sent out their first equally tempered organs. This must therefore be considered as the commercial date for equal temperament on new organs in England. On old organs meantone temperament lingered much later. In 1880, when I [Ellis] wrote my *History of Musical Pitch*, from which most of these particulars have been taken, I found meantone temperament still general in Spain, and used in England on Greene's three organs, at St. George's Chapel, Windsor (since altered), at St. Katharine's, Regent's Park, and at Kew Parish Church; and while many others had only recently been altered, one (Jordan's at Maidstone Old Parish Church) was being altered when I visited it in that year. Hence, in England, equal temperament, though now (1883) firmly established, is not quite 40 years old on the pianoforte, and only 30 years old on the organ.

Alexander J. Ellis, "Additions by the Translator,"
in On the Sensations of Tone (1885)[4]

From this gratifyingly detailed account we learn of the gradual introduction of ET into England around 1850, first for pianos, then for organs. Although Ellis found meantone organs in general use in Spain and in scattered use throughout England around 1880, he could still describe ET as "firmly established" in 1883. "Firmly established" is, of course, not the same thing as a universal standard. I remember being startled, many years ago, hearing fortepiano collector E. Michael Frederick say that he possessed tuning instructions by someone in the Erard piano firm from around 1910, and that the temperament described was not ET. I used to tell people that story and they would always ask, "Really? What was it?" For a long time I never knew. I finally contacted Mike and Patricia Frederick for the reference, which turned out to be an article on the piano in the *Encyclopédie de la Musique et Dictionnaire du Conservatoire* of 1913, written by Alphonse Blondel. Blondel had become head of the Erard piano firm in 1873, and in that 1913 article the tuning he recommended as "harmonious and possessed of a charm which makes plain the natural qualities of the instrument" was one that used five tempered fifths and seven pure ones, much the same kind of building blocks for a temperament as irregular systems from the eighteenth century. Since the five tempered fifths were tuned alike, we can determine that they were narrow by about one-fifth of a comma. Blondel's approach was different from most historical temperaments, however, since he interspersed tempered and pure fifths in the series, rather than concentrating most of the tempered fifths in a row in order to favor those keys. There were historical precedents for such a system, however, since in 1790 theorist and composer Friedrich Wilhelm Marpurg had described a temperament with alternating tempered and pure fifths, though using six of each rather than five tempered and seven pure fifths.* And there is evidence that temperaments like that were used in practice well into the twentieth century. Not all early piano recordings are clear enough and free enough from wow and flutter to allow frequency analysis, but the May 26, 1924, recording of Chopin's Prélude op. 28, no. 15 in D♭ by Chopin specialist Vladimir de Pachmann† seems clearly to reveal a temperament based on such an alternation of narrow and wide fifths.

So while ET was, to use Ellis's term, "firmly established," we can hardly describe it as the only thing that musicians were using, even into the twentieth century. We may further question whether the temperament people were describing as ET in the nineteenth

---

*Neue Methode allerley Arten von Temperaturen dem Claviere aufs Bequemste mitzutheilen (Berlin, 1790), tenth temperament, pp. 30–31. There are precedents for this kind of scheme (though using larger fractions of the comma and more pure fifths) as far back as Johann Philipp Bendeler's Organopoeia in 1690.

†Vladimir de Pachmann, Opal CD #9840 (1989), track 3 (though described in the accompanying booklet as track 2). Pachmann was the first pianist born before 1850 to be substantially represented in recording catalogs. His first session was in 1907.

Alexander Ellis

Alexander J. Ellis (né John Sharpe), the English philologist and mathematician, was born in Hoxton, near London, on June 14, 1814, and died in London on October 28, 1890. He changed his surname because of a legacy from a relative named Ellis, which gave him the means to work as an independent scholar for the rest of his life. Educated at Eton and Cambridge, he was known first as a mathematician, but then became an important philologist—in fact, the first great scholar of English pronunciation. With Sir Isaac Pitman (of Pitman Shorthand fame) during the 1840s, he essentially devised the basis of modern phonetics. His publications on pronunciation, besides the more general *Pronunciation for Singers* (1877), include *On Early English Pronunciation, with Especial Reference to Shakespeare and Chaucer* (1869). Part 5 of that work was abridged and published separately as *English Dialects—Their Sounds and Homes* (1890), showing Ellis's passion for contemporary English dialects that had made him—as Shaw acknowledged—a prototype for Professor Henry Higgins in *Pygmalion* (later *My Fair Lady*), first published in 1916. As Shaw reminisced in the Preface: "When I became interested in [phonetics] towards the end of the eighteen-seventies, . . . Alexander J. Ellis was still a living patriarch, with an impressive head always covered by a velvet skull cap, for which he would apologize to public meetings in a very courtly manner." Intrigued by the pitch of vocal sounds, Ellis studied music in Edinburgh and became a writer on scientific aspects of music, beginning with his first translation of Helmholtz in 1875. His work on the

Alexander J. Ellis "as I remember him" according to George Bernard Shaw in 1949.

musical scales of various nations has caused him to be widely recognized as the father of the field of ethnomusicology. His essay "On the History of Musical Pitch" (1880) is another landmark publication, and the basis of more recent studies by Arthur Mendel and Bruce Haynes. In that work, Ellis noted that, in the spirit of scientific inquiry, he had "purposely relied on mechanical evaluation, to the exclusion of mere estimation of ear." Indeed, he was modest about his own musical ability, although it is very unlikely that he was really "tone-deaf," as A. J. Hipkins's daughter Edith affectionately described him decades later.

century was really ET. Indeed, Owen Jorgensen, one of today's leading authorities on historical temperaments, regards 1917 as the "before and after" date in the history of temperament:

> After 1917, tempering became a skilled science based on universally accepted mathematical principles, and professional tuners now temper with similar results. There is little individuality, and the temperament sections of pianos tuned by different tuners match note for note when compared.
>
> Before 1917, tempering was an art based on a keen sense of color awareness for each individual interval or chord on the piano. This color sense that was developed through environmental conditioning by listening to tunings and piano music during the nineteenth century is now lost. Wise aesthetic decisions based on classical traditions are no longer being made. Indeed, such judgments are contrary to twentieth-century atonal philosophy.
>
> Owen Jorgensen, Tuning (1991)[5]

The 1917 turning point Jorgensen refers to is the publication date of William Braid White's *Modern Piano Tuning and Allied Arts.* White (1878–1959) was a Cambridge-educated acoustical engineer who emigrated to the United States in 1898 and, with his 1917 manual, basically founded the science of truly equal tempered piano tuning. His process of counting beats and of using "checks" (comparative intervals) throughout the process made it finally possible to ensure that the temperament was truly equal throughout. Before 1917 they may have called it ET, they may have thought they were tuning ET, but they weren't. Even as far back as 1864, many years before his comments in the Helmholtz translation, Ellis worried that ET wasn't really ET:

> [ET] is, however, so difficult to realize by the ordinary methods of tuning, that "equal temperament" . . . has probably never been attained in this country, with any approach to mathematical precision.
>
> Alexander J. Ellis, "On the Temperament of Musical Instruments with Fixed Tones" (1864)[6]

William Braid White

William Braid White was born in England in 1878 and died in the United States in 1959. He was educated as an acoustical engineer at Cambridge before emigrating in 1898. Six years later he became the technical editor of the *Music Trade Review* in New York, a post he held for nearly thirty years. In 1910 he founded the American Guild of Piano Tuners, the forerunner of today's Piano Technicians Guild. His seminal *Modern Piano Tuning and Allied Arts* appeared in 1917. During the 1920s he was central to the establishment of A = 440 as the modern pitch standard. After a stint as an acoustical engineer at the American Steel and Wire Company (a subsidiary of U.S. Steel), he became technical editor of *Piano Trade Magazine* in 1938. He was also the founder and longtime principal of the School of Pianoforte Technology in Chicago. Braid White was undoubtedly the foremost piano technician of the twentieth century.

William Braid White in 1930 "photographing" noise in Chicago. (Underwood & Underwood/Corbis)

Ellis had first translated Helmholtz's third edition (1870) in 1875. By the time of his translation of Helmholtz's expanded fourth and last edition (1877) in 1885, Ellis had become fascinated with what tuners were really doing, so he set up an experiment to find out. He used an instrument called a tonometer, consisting of 105 precisely calibrated tuning forks covering a range of about an octave and a fourth. By comparing musical notes with that instrument, he was able to measure their frequencies to an accuracy of about two decimal places—a remarkable degree of precision. He then set up an experiment analyzing the work of the finest tuners of the 1880s in England, identifying their previously ET-tuned instruments or commissioning them to tune ET anew. This is how he described each of the lines in his chart of results:

Line 1. The theoretical intervals, all exact hundreds of cents.
Line 2. My own piano, tuned by one of Broadwood's usual tuners, and let stand unused for a fortnight.
Lines 3, 4, 5. Three grand pianos by Broadwoods' best tuners, prepared for examination through the kindness of Mr. A. J. Hipkins, of that house.
Line 6. An organ tuned a week previously by one of Mr. T. Hill's tuners, and used only once, examined by the kind permissions of Mr. G. Hickson, treasurer of South Place Chapel, Finsbury, where the organ stood.
Line 7. An harmonium tuned by one of the Messrs. Moore & Moore tuners, kindly prepared for my examination.
Line 8. An harmonium, used as a standard of pitch, tuned a year previously by Mr. D. J. Blaikley, by means of accurately counted beats, &c., with a constant blast, put at my disposal for examination by Mr. Blaikley.

Alexander J. Ellis, "Additions by the Translator,"
in On the Sensations of Tone (1885)[7]

The first line uses a term familiar to anyone experienced in discussions of temperament, but one I have not used here before:

HOW EQUAL TEMPERAMENT RUINED HARMONY

cents. Each cent, in fact, represents one one-hundredth of an ET semitone. It's a very useful unit of measure, but I chose not to use it in this book until now because, in fact, it was introduced by Ellis in 1885. Up to that point people still thought in terms of fractions of a comma, and so on, so those are the terms that I have used. Now that we have encountered cents as part of Ellis's discussion, they will form part of our analytic arsenal from here on. The simple thing to remember is that there are 100 cents in every ET semitone, and therefore 1200 cents in every octave. Thus, the ET whole tone is 200c, the ET major third is 400c, and the ET fifth is 700c, and so on. These compare, by the way, with the acoustically pure fifth at 701.96c and the acoustically pure major third at 386.31c, slightly wider and much narrower, respectively, than their ET counterparts.

Central to the piano tuning in Ellis's list above is Alfred J. Hipkins, who has already been mentioned in connection with the introduction of ET into England at the Broadwood piano firm. Besides being head of tuning at Broadwood's, Hipkins was a concert pianist as well as an historian of musical instruments. He himself was, in fact, the tuner of choice for Frédéric Chopin when the legendary composer-pianist was in Britain, so his authority and skill in tuning pianos was unsurpassed. The fact that he handpicked the tuners for Ellis's experiment suggests that he chose the very best that England had to offer, and thus the results of their versions of ET are all the more interesting.

The results of Ellis's tuners were not ET, even though that is what the tuners were asked to do and what they presumably believed they were doing. In a series of twelve fifths, ET fifths would each appear as 700c, slightly narrow from pure fifths at close to 702c. Owen Jorgensen took the results of the five best of Ellis's tuners, averaged them, and gave the results as follows:[8]

C	G	D	A	E	B	F♯	C♯	G♯/A♭	E♭	B♭	F	C
700.7	698.5	698.4	698.6	701.4	700.9	700.5	700.4	699.4	700.7	699.9	700.6	

Alfred J. Hipkins

Alfred J. Hipkins was born at Westminster in central London on June 17, 1826, and died in nearby Kensington on June 3, 1903. He apprenticed as a piano tuner at Broadwood's when he was fourteen and remained with the firm for more than sixty years. This devotion to the piano notwithstanding, he was also one of the first to revive the playing of early keyboard instruments, performing on clavichord and harpsichord at the Musical Association in 1886. On piano he was known as an insightful interpreter of Chopin (as well as Chopin's tuner of choice when he was in London). Hipkins was not only an extensive contributor to George Grove's original *Dictionary of Music and Musicians* (1890), and musical consultant for the *Oxford English Dictionary*, but his *Description and History of the Pianoforte* (London, 1896) confirmed him as a leading authority on the subject of keyboard instruments. His beautifully illustrated *Musical Instruments: Historic, Rare and Unique* (Edinburgh, 1888) included historical—even ancient—European instruments of all types, and also demonstrated the author's wide knowledge of non-Western instruments, including examples from India, China, Japan, and

South Africa. Hipkins was honorary curator of the Royal College of Music, to which he bequeathed his own collection of instruments.

Alfred J. Hipkins at the harpsichord. Portrait by his daughter, Edith (1898). (National Portrait Gallery, London)

Vladimir de Pachmann

The pianist Vladimir de Pachmann was born in Odessa, Ukraine, on July 27, 1848, and died in Rome on January 6, 1933. After lessons with his father, a distinguished Austrian amateur violinist, Vladimir studied at the Vienna Conservatory with Joseph Dachs, receiving the gold medal in 1869. He began concertizing but was so awed on hearing Polish pianist Karl Tausig play in Odessa in 1870 that he left the stage for eight more years of private preparation.

Eventually Pachmann became renowned as an interpreter of Chopin, especially, but also of miniatures by composers like Schumann and Mendelssohn. In part because of his unconventional manner, Pachmann became a celebrity throughout Europe and America. He made his debut in London in 1882 and in America in 1890. After farewell concerts in New York in 1925 and London in 1928, he retired to Italy.

Pachmann's reputation for eccentricity, especially his compulsive talking to the audience during recitals, has largely overshadowed his reputation as a player. The more he talked, however, the more it was expected, and the more it happened. But many experts, including Kaikhosru Sorabji (himself an eccentric virtuoso), agreed that Pachmann's best work showed

incomparable nuance and delicacy. An archive of his recordings is housed at the Gustafson Piano Library in Lennoxville, Quebec.

Vladimir de Pachmann at the piano, from a Baldwin Piano Company advertisement (1925). (Author's collection)

What is especially striking about this averaged late-nineteenth-century temperament—so-called ET but not really—is how much it resembles "well temperaments" of the eighteenth century. The result of concentrating so much of the tempering of the fifths in the notes G through E is to favor the most common chords in the most common keys. So while these tuners thought they were tuning ET, in reality, whether unconsciously or consciously, they were shading the temperament toward the keys they knew would probably be used most often. This is lip service to an ET ideal while doing something else, and yet this is indisputably what the "best" tuners were doing ca. 1885. After the publication of Braid White's tuning method in 1917, though Pachmann's recording shows that a few, perhaps, older musicians continued to use unequal systems, it's clear that tuners could no longer fool themselves into thinking they were tuning ET when they were really favoring some keys over others.

Piano collector E. Michael Frederick, who has devoted a great deal of his life to studying and restoring pianos from this era, objects to the view that this deviation from ET is significant.* He is absolutely right that differences from modern performance techniques in pedaling, tempo, articulation, ornamentation, and so on, would probably be more immediately obvious to the listener, but still, tuners thought they were tuning ET before 1917, and they almost certainly were not. And the differences, though subtle, grow more significant on repeated hearings.

*This view is expressed in an essay, "Some Thoughts on Equal Temperament Tuning," graciously sent to me by Mr. Frederick.

CHAPTER EIGHT

The "Joachim Mode"

Such, with its faults and its merits, is the scale system accepted at the present time in countries the most advanced in civilisation. It is called the equal temperament. Thus, pianos and organs are tuned, and all instruments having fixed tones. Stringed instruments, voices, and in certain cases, wind instruments are able to make the enharmonic notes differ.

ALBERT LAVIGNAC, Music and Musicians (1895)[1]

I HAVE SPENT quite a lot of time going over what piano tuners were doing—or thought they were doing—in the late nineteenth and early twentieth centuries. It's time to turn to the issue of non-keyboard tuning during the same period. One of the best subjects for this purpose is Joseph Joachim. He was a figure of towering importance among violinists in the nineteenth century, described in the first edition of Grove's *Dictionary of Music and Musicians* in 1890, as "the greatest of living violin-players" and "a master of technique, surpassed by no one."[2] Born in 1831, he made his concert debut before his eighth birthday. At the age of eleven, he began studying with Felix Mendelssohn, who shortly thereafter took him to London to play the Beethoven Violin Concerto. After Mendelssohn's death Joachim, while still in his teens, became Franz Liszt's concertmaster in Weimar. In the following years, he became a friend and collaborator of the Schumanns and Brahms,

Joseph Joachim

Joseph Joachim, the Austro-Hungarian violinist, composer, conductor, and teacher, was born near Bratislava on June 28, 1831, and died in Berlin on August 15, 1907. In 1833 his family moved from Slovakia to Pest (later part of Budapest). He studied in Vienna with Joseph Böhm, a former pupil of Pierre Rode, himself taught by Giovanni Battista Viotti, both of whom were mainstays of the classical French school of violin playing.

By the time he was twelve, Joachim's technique had fully matured, and by 1843 he was studying with Mendelssohn in Leipzig, becoming only the second person to play Mendelssohn's new Concerto for Violin. The composer took the boy to London, where, in May 1844, his playing of Beethoven's Violin Concerto was a sensation. The work became one of his signature pieces

Joseph Joachim in 1903. (Johanna Eilert, Copyright Lebrecht Music & Arts)

and he performed it more often than any other, except for the Chaconne from Bach's D Minor solo Partita.

After Mendelssohn's death in 1847, Joachim went to study with Liszt in Weimar. Like Mendelssohn, Liszt's teaching included considerable performing with the young man, and encouraging his composing. In Weimar, Joachim began also to explore the chamber repertory, one early highlight being a performance of Beethoven's Kreutzer Sonata with Hans von Bülow in 1852. From 1853 to 1868, Joachim was principal violinist at the Hannover court, but toured internationally and established his first string quartet. He developed a close friendship with the Schumanns and Brahms, and consequently rejected the musical path of his former teacher, Liszt, and the so-called New German School. He also converted from Judaism to Lutheranism.

In 1868, Joachim moved to Berlin, where he established a school that continues to this day as the Hochschule für Musik at the University of the Arts. Joachim put such emphasis on quartet playing that he seems to have been the first to offer recitals entirely devoted to them, presenting the complete repertory from Haydn to Brahms. In addition, many concertos were written for him, including those by Schumann, Brahms, Bruch, and Dvořák. His own violin concertos are so daunting technically that, in spite of their musical merit, they are rarely performed today. This only helps to confirm his reputation as one of the greatest violinists of all time.

and an influential teacher, founding in 1868 what is now the Hochschule für Musik at the University of the Arts in Berlin.

There are several ways in which Joachim's playing contributes to the discussion of temperament in the late nineteenth century. The first occurs in 1863, when Helmholtz reports a temperament experiment modeled after that of Delezenne in 1827:

> That performers of the first rank do really play in just intonation has been directly proved by the very interesting and exact results of Delezenne. This observer determined the individual notes of the major scale, as it was played by distinguished violinists and violoncellists, by means of an accurately gauged string, and found that these players produced correctly perfect Thirds and Sixths, and neither equally tempered nor Pythagorean Thirds or Sixths. I was fortunate enough to have an opportunity of making similar observations by means of my harmonium on Herr Joachim. He tuned his violin exactly with the $g \pm d \pm a \pm e$ of my instrument. I then requested him to play the scale, and immediately he had played the Third or Sixth, I gave the corresponding note on the harmonium. By means of beats it was easy to determine that this distinguished musician used b_1 and not b as the major Third to g, and e_1 not e as the Sixth.
>
> Hermann von Helmholtz, *Die Lehre den Tonempfindungen als physiologische Grundlage für die Theorie der Musik* (1863)[3]

Helmholtz here reports that Joachim, playing his violin unaccompanied, placed the third and sixth notes of a G major scale pure to the starting note. This Helmholtz checked by comparing Joachim's notes with a harmonium, or reed organ, tuned in Just intonation. This implies that Joachim preferred pure major and minor thirds when not forced to temper them—as when he played with a piano, for example. I find it surprising that a violin virtuoso in the 1860s would come anywhere near a pure major third in a scale. Helmholtz was a great scientist, but I wonder if he got the results he hoped for in that situation, or if Joachim knew what Helmholtz wanted and graciously obliged. Still, Helmholtz's observations are interesting in the light of what happens later, and may stand as our first inklings of the "Joachim mode."

Helmholtz's results may also be usefully contrasted with the experiments of Alexander Ellis on melodic vs. harmonic tuning by amateur and professional string players, published in Ellis's first edition of his Helmholtz translation in 1875.[4] The Belgian violinist, M. (Hubert) Léonard played eleven major thirds which average 408.98c, slightly larger even than a Pythagorean ditone. His minor third averages to 292.95c, which almost perfectly fills out a pure fifth when combined with his major third. The cellist M. (Hyppolyte Prosper) Séligmann averaged his eight major thirds at 406.6c, slightly smaller than a ditone but still much larger than ET. His minor third averages to 301.86c, which is slightly wider than ET. Violinist M. (Albert) Ferrand of the Opéra Comique played major thirds that average 402.36c and minor thirds that average 301.7c. The two violinists, furthermore, played leading notes that average 77.4c, which is extraordinarily narrow. Clearly some professional string players were leaning toward the higher leading notes, wide major thirds, and narrow minor thirds of ET, and that in some cases go beyond even Pythagorean proportions. (A normal Pythagorean leading note, for example, is 90.22c.)

Evidence suggests that Joachim continued to follow his own path, however. When the distinguished violinist was in his late fifties, George Bernard Shaw heard him in London and reacted very negatively to what he heard.

28 *February* 1890

I was lucky in looking in to hear Joachim at the Popular Concert last Monday. I must first mention, however, that Joachim was never to me an Orpheus. Like all the pupils of Mendelssohn he has seldom done anything with an *allegro* except try to make speed do duty for meaning. Now that he is on the verge of sixty he keeps up the speed at the cost of quality of tone and accuracy of pitch; and the results are sometimes, to say the least, incongruous. For instance, he played Bach's sonata in C at the Bach Choir Concert at St. James's Hall on Tuesday. The second movement of that work is a fugue some three or four hundred bars long. Of course you cannot really play a fugue in three continuous parts on the violin; but by dint of doublestopping and dodging from one part to another, you can evoke a hideous ghost of a fugue that will pass current if guaranteed by Bach and Joachim. That was what happened on Tuesday. Joachim scraped away frantically, making a sound after which an attempt to grate a nutmeg effectively on a boot sole would have been as the strain of an Aeolian harp. The notes which were musical enough to have any discernible pitch at all were mostly out of tune. It was horrible—damnable! Had he been an unknown player, introducing an unknown composer, he would not have escaped with his life. Yet we all—I no less than the others—were interested and enthusiastic. We applauded like anything; and he bowed to us with unimpaired gravity. The dignified artistic career of Joachim and the grandeur of Bach's reputation had so hypnotized us that we took an abominable noise for the music of the spheres.

George Bernard Shaw, London Music in 1888–89 as Heard by Corno di Bassetto (Later Known as Bernard Shaw) with Some Further Autobiographical Particulars (1937)[5]

Shaw's report is amusing but seems nonetheless a terrible indictment of Joachim's playing, leading us to believe that his skills had sadly diminished or that he was having a *very* bad day. Something about Joachim's playing was gnawing at Shaw, and it took a subsequent concert for him to identify it. Just over three years later, Shaw heard Joachim again and came to the conclusion that he really was a superb master of the instrument but that he had a different concept of temperament from what Shaw himself preferred.

HOW EQUAL TEMPERAMENT RUINED HARMONY

Joachim perfecting his nutmeg
and boot-sole imitation

29 *March* 1893

I seldom go to a Monday Popular Concert without wondering how many people who sit out the quartets and sonatas feel the heavy responsibility which they incur as the dispensers of applause and success to young artists. Last Monday week I heard them give a tremendous ovation to Joachim, who had played Bach's Chaconne in D minor, and played it, certainly, with a fineness of tone and a perfect dignity of style and fitness of phrasing that can fairly be described as magnificent. If the intonation had only had the exquisite natural justice of Sarasate's, instead of the austerity of that peculiar scale which may be called the Joachim mode, and which is tempered according to Joachim's temperament and not according to that of the sunny South, I should have confidently said to my neighbor that this particular performance could never be surpassed by mortal violinist.

But the thought that the miracle of miracles might arrive in the shape of a violinist with Sarasate's intonation and Joachim's style made me forbear. This peculiar intonation of Joachim's for a long time greatly hindered my appreciation of his art: the Celtic troll in me rebelled against intervals that were not the same as my intervals. For I may as well make known, as a remarkable discovery in psychical physics, that the modes in which we express ourselves musically, that is, the major and minor scales, though in theory series of sounds bearing a fixed pitch relation to one another, are in practice tempered by every musician just as the proportions of the human figure are tempered by a sculptor. Some physicist should make a tonometer giving a theoretically perfect major scale, in order that Joachim, Sarasate, Ysaÿe, and Reményi should have an opportunity of hearing how far the four different tone figures which they have made for themselves as major scales differ from the theoretic scale and from one another. Only the worst of it is that the tonometer would probably turn out to be inaccurate, as scientific instruments usually are.

Schumann's metronome led him a pretty dance; and Appun's tonometer bothered the late Alexander J. Ellis handsomely until it occurred to him that a box of reeds was much more likely to get out of condition than the organ of Corti inside the head of a musician. Still, the fact that a tonometer is quite as likely as a violinist to set up a scale peculiar to its individual self does not affect my contention that every artist modifies the scale to suit his own ear; that every nation does the same; and that the musical critic of the future, instead of crudely saying, as I do, that the Germans have every musical qualification except ear, will classify the national and individual modes, and dispassionately announce that the intonation of So-and-So, the new virtuoso, is German-lymphatic, or Spanish-bilious, or English-evangelical, or what not. And he will train himself to tolerate and appreciate all these different modes, just as I have come to such a perfect toleration of Joachim's that I no longer have the least feeling that he is playing out of tune except when he is false to his own scale.

I submit this enlightened attitude for the imitation of those rash persons who accuse Joachim of playing out of tune, and whose standard of intonation is often founded on the luscious strains of the accordion as made in Italy, or on keyed instruments like the common pianoforte, with its sharp thirds, flat fifths, and generally tinkered and compromised tuning. Even if Joachim played every note out of tune, the quality of his tone and the thoroughness of his interpretation would compel us to listen to him, though we groaned with anguish at every stroke of the bow.

George Bernard Shaw, *Music in London, 1890–1894* (1932)[6]

Interesting that in 1893 Shaw would comment on the "compromised" tuning of the piano. Shaw was, of course, a gifted writer and sensitive listener, but he was not a professional musician. One person in an excellent position to have an insider's opinion on Joachim's artistry was Donald Francis Tovey. Tovey's name is known to posterity for his insightful essays on musical analysis and for his perceptive encyclopedia articles, but he was himself an extraordinary pianist, and after hearing Joachim first at the age of seven, he actually performed with him several times, beginning at the age of eighteen in 1894. Tovey realized that Joachim had lost some technical ground due to age:

> . . . there are many fairly musical persons of various ages who know just enough to feel pleasure and pain in music and who have no conception of ensemble beyond that of never failing to play exactly together. In consequence, they are disturbed beyond measure by the slightest accident that shows that a performer is not a machine, infallible because lifeless and inhuman. And so it comes to pass that many of Dr. Joachim's admirers, for lack of more positive ideas about musical technique and expression, find themselves unreasonably worried by the unmusical statistics which are cited to prove by rule of three that a great artist at the age of 71 is not so young as he was thirty years ago.
>
> Donald Francis Tovey, "The Joachim Quartet" (1902)[7]

In this same review, Tovey expresses the view that "Everyone who has an idea of the positive qualities of a perfect ensemble will agree that that of the Joachim Quartet is as perfect as any artistic unity that we can conceive," and further, that "the Joachim Quartet possesses a technique that is beyond the dreams of virtuosity." Tovey's emphasis on the less soloistic, chamber music orientation of Joachim was a theme revisited in his 1907 obituary of the violinist, in which he says:

> To most of us, especially to the younger generation, the idea most closely associated with the name of Joachim is not that of a great solo player, but of the ruling spirit of a quartet of players, the other three of whom shared his ideals in all things and drew inspiration from him.
>
> Donald Francis Tovey, "Joseph Joachim" (1907)[8]

But, of course, Joachim was not just a quartet leader. He consulted on the composition of, premiered, or was the dedicatee of violin concertos by Schumann, Bruch, Dvořák, and Brahms, among others (as well as giving the second performance of the Mendelssohn concerto), and his interpretation of Beethoven's

HOW EQUAL TEMPERAMENT RUINED HARMONY

Violin Concerto simply set the standard for the century. In addition his renditions of the unaccompanied sonatas and partitas of Bach brought those pieces for the first time into the mainstream of the violin repertory. My reading of all this is that Joseph Joachim, steeped in the harmonic priorities of string quartet playing, never adapted to the newer, soloistic style of higher leading notes that was becoming more and more prevalent through the latter part of the nineteenth century. Was "the Joachim mode," as coined by George Bernard Shaw, a more harmonic, less linear conception of tuning, one opposed to the high leading notes of ET and the evolving soloistic style? As it turns out, yes.

Joachim was the earliest of the major violinists to make recordings, so the third way in which he contributes to our discussion is through his 1903 recordings. Though exhibiting technical imperfections that would never be tolerated in a performance or recording today (something characteristic of most of these very early recordings), and though marred by constant hiss and a rudimentary recording process, Joachim's approach is audibly instructive. But by importing his performances, now all available on CD, into a frequency-counting program, it is possible to take precise, scientific measurements of the intervals he used. There are still problems with this: The equipment was so unsteady that the frequencies of any sustained sound change over the course of the note; and even in a modern CD, variations in bow pressure can cause minute fluctuations in pitch. But there is enough in Joachim's recordings to determine by listening alone that his major thirds tend to be narrower than in ET, and to confirm that by counting frequencies, particularly in simultaneous sonorities. At m. 15 in the first movement Adagio of Bach's G Minor Sonata, a prominent G–B major third can be measured at 389.26c, and the minor third in the final chord is 313.36c. These are not exactly pure major and minor thirds (which would be 386.31c and 315.64c), but they are quite close, especially when compared with the ET intervals at 400c and 300c, respectively. In his recording of the Gavotte from Bach's B Minor Partita, there is one very prominent diminished fifth that measures at 605.95c, which compares with the pure interval at 609.78c—again, not pure but much closer than the ET counterpart at 600c.*

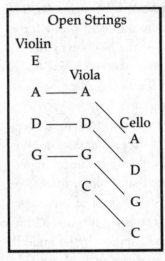

Figure 16. Violin Family Tuning.

In order to maintain that Joachim was attempting to come somewhere close to such a system, one critical clue would be his placement of the open strings. If his open strings are pure—which is to say, even wider than in ET—it would be clear that a system using narrower major thirds, wider minor thirds, and so on, would not be the goal. The reason for this should be easy to see. Figure 16 shows the open strings of the violin family of instruments.

If all the open strings are tuned pure (702c), then the A–C minor third between the outer strings of both the cello and viola—tuned identically though an octave apart—will be quite narrow at 294c. This is because the three comparatively wide fifths (C–G, G–D, D–A) push the A quite high and thus closer to the C. The greatest cost, however, will be the major third between the bottom C string of the cello/viola and the top E string of the violin: It will be a Pythagorean major third, or ditone (408c), even wider than ET

---

*What is especially interesting about this, as noted above, is that one characteristic of extended-sixth-comma meantone is that the tritone and diminished fifth are pure. In fact Ellis refers to sixth-comma meantone as the "True Tritonic" system. See Ellis, "Additions by the Translator," in *On the Sensations of Tone* (1885), pp. 547–48.

and much too wide for most players' tolerance, even today. The fact is, high leading notes, wide major thirds, and the wide open-string fifths necessary to achieve them simply make the harmony unbearable. One passage notorious for testing the tuning of open strings in this way is the following from Beethoven's String Quartet, op. 127.

Ex. 3. Beethoven String Quartet no. 12 in E♭ Major, op. 127, first mvt., mm. 135–37.

Here the cello and viola both must play their low C and G on open strings. The second violinist, meanwhile, must play an open string E because the second string is occupied with the C. (Otherwise, it would be possible to play an E on the second string and play it a little lower so that it was better harmonically.) Furthermore, since the dynamic is fortissimo, the effect of the wide C–E major third created by pure (or nearly pure) open-string fifths is exacerbated, and this normally causes players to consider narrowing their fifths somewhat from pure. Though still not very pleasant, an ET major third would be a slight improvement, and could be achieved by narrowing each of the four fifths (C–G, G–D, D–A, A–E) by two cents, resulting in a C–E third of exactly 400c. This is presumably what most string players do today. If, on the other hand, Joachim's goal in 1903 was a major third that is harmonically *better* than ET, then we should expect to find him tuning his open strings even narrower than in ET, and we do.

In Bach's B Minor Bourrée, comparing chords that absolutely require open strings suggests that Joachim is tuning the violin's unstopped notes as follows:

A–E	698.09c
D–A	700.35c
G–D	697.41c

These three average to 698.62c, which comes remarkably close to sixth-comma meantone at 698.37c. In the Adagio of Bach's G Minor Sonata, Joachim's open strings appear to be tuned as follows:

A–E	700.39c
D–A	697.50c
G–D	698.98c

These three average to open string fifths of 698.96c. Whether the slight differences are intentional and perhaps based on the key of the pieces is unclear, but the overall result is very similar. The really striking thing about these figures, however, is how well they match with the averaged fifths for the open-string notes among Ellis's "best" piano tuners, cited earlier:

A–E	698.6c
D–A	698.4c
G–D	698.5c
C–G	700.7c

G–D–A–E—the open strings of the violin—average to 698.5c, but including the viola and cello's C–G fifth as well, gives an overall average for the open strings of 699.05c, which comes to within a tenth of a cent (1/1000 of a semitone) of the figures from Joachim's playing.

All of this reinforces my belief that while the trend, especially among virtuosic solo players, was toward higher leading notes—ET and beyond—there was still a strong tradition of playing harmonies that favored the more euphonious major and minor thirds of the long-standard ensemble tuning system—essentially a continuation of the extended-sixth-comma or 55-division system described again and again in the eighteenth century.* This may have been most prevalent among those who, like Joachim, were committed players of string quartets and the like, where the piano's tendency toward ET, and the linear demands of the soloist toward higher and higher leading notes, could more easily be resisted—indeed *had* to be resisted in the interests of the priority of the harmony. Lower major thirds in a triad mean wider diatonic leading notes, and those intervals must be answered in any system by wider minor thirds and narrower chromatic semitones. The inescapable conclusion is that some of the best performers, even into the early twentieth century, did not use ET.

In fact, while Joachim was clearly avoiding ET in favor of a more harmonic approach, the evidence shows that some performers were heading in the opposite direction, using wide major thirds and narrow leading notes. In his 1904 recording of the Prélude from Bach's E Major Partita, Pablo de Sarasate—Shaw's ideal for intonation, remember—plays one chord with an average major third of 406.33c. Casals's "expressive intonation," it appears, had antecedents in Spain. My guess is that Sarasate's high leading notes, whether harmonic or melodic, would cause

*It may have seemed odd that the meantone and extended-meantone systems shown in figures 6 and 9 are centered on D, rather than on C. In fact this fits beautifully with string instruments, since D sits in the exact center of the open strings of the violin family: C–G–D–A–E.

Pablo de Sarasate

Pablo de Sarasate, the virtuoso violinist and composer, was born in Pamplona, Spain, on March 10, 1844, and died in Biarritz on September 20, 1908. The son of a military band conductor, he began violin at five, performing publicly for the first time when he was eight. Sponsored by Queen Isabella of Spain, he studied at the Paris Conservatoire beginning in 1856, winning prizes in violin, solfège, and harmony. He then began the concert tours that made him famous all over the Western world, from Europe

Pablo de Sarasate. (Copyright Lebrecht Music & Arts)

even modern violinists who *like* high leading notes to raise their eyebrows, if not to actually rise up out of their seats. The cost of these high leading notes—the cost of favoring the linear direction of the melodic line over the vertical sonority—simply put, is the quality of the harmony. Sarasate's leading notes are *really* high, but even ET's wide major thirds are high enough to ruin the harmony by the standards of many, many professional composers and musicians up to the early twentieth century.

Perhaps the most ironic documentation for the trend toward high leading notes, however, comes from Alphonse Blondel, whom we have already seen advocating non-ET piano tuning in 1913:

to South America. Sarasate was liked and admired by many famous composers who dedicated concertos to him, including Bruch, Saint-Saëns, Lalo, and Wieniawski. After his Vienna debut in 1876, he enjoyed considerable success in the German-speaking countries—all the more remarkable since his style was so different from that of Joachim, Germany's acknowledged master. Indeed, to Sarasate's annoyance, his interpretation of the Beethoven concerto was sometimes compared unfavorably with Joachim's.

Sarasate's recordings reveal his tone to be sweet and pure, produced with a smooth bowstroke and a fast but narrow vibrato. His technique was confident, and his whole manner of playing was effortless to the point of nonchalance. Sarasate left his two Stradivarius violins to conservatory museums: His favorite (dated 1724) went to Paris and the other, the so-called Boissier (1713), to Madrid.

The musical sound called the whole tone is divided ideally into nine parts called *commas*, four of these forming the diatonic semitone, and five the chromatic semitone, so that, for example, C♯ is a comma higher than D♭.

Alphonse Blondel, "Le Piano et sa Facture,"
in Encyclopédie de la Musique et
Dictionnaire du Conservatoire (1913)[9]

Here we have the vocabulary of the 55-division system used in reverse to rationalize "expressive intonation."* Well, at least it

---

*The 55-division vocabulary it may be, but using the smaller, four-comma interval as the diatonic semitone means that Blondel's octave is made up of only 53

Alphonse Blondel

Alphonse Blondel was head of the venerable Erard piano manufacturing firm in Paris from 1873. He died in 1935. Blondel was a contributor to the *Encyclopédie de la Musique et Dictionnaire du Conservatoire* (Paris, 1913). As a piano maker he resisted the new cross-strung American design, maintaining that the old, straight-strung model produced a better tone. His company had to conform to the new standard eventually, however, since the Erard sound was softer and lighter

Alphonse Blondel in 1911 from Pianos and Their Makers, *by Alfred Dolge (1911–13).*

than the newer design, and balance with large symphony orchestras had become an important issue for soloists.

Interestingly Blondel always styled himself A. Blondel, and perhaps because of that ambiguity he appears in some histories as Albert-Louis Blondel. It is not known whether Alphonse Blondel the piano maker is identical with the eponymous founder of the pioneering French athletic association, Club des Coureurs, in 1875.

---

commas rather than 55: Five whole tones ($5 \times 9 = 45$ commas) plus two diatonic—in this case, small—semitones ($2 \times 4 = 8$ commas) = 53 commas. The 53-division comma is also larger than the 55-division one, since 1200/53 (22.64 cents) is larger than 1200/55 (21.82 cents).

shows that the idea of a whole tone of nine commas was still alive in 1913, and nine commas cannot be arranged into two equal semitones. However dominant ET may have grown by the second decade of the twentieth century, it wasn't the only system in existence . . . yet.

CHAPTER NINE

"The Limbo of That Which Is Disregarded"

> *By constantly listening to the equally tempered scale, the ear may be brought, not only to tolerate its intervals, but to prefer them to those of any other system, at least as far as melody is concerned.*
>
> JAMES LECKY, "Temperament," in *A Dictionary of Music and Musicians* (1890)[1]

IT'S WORTH CONSIDERING how it was that ET was embraced so completely, first as an ideal after the middle of the nineteenth century, then as a universal standard after 1917. So complete, in fact, has been the adoption of ET that most musicians today are not even aware that any other systems exist, or if they exist, that they have any musical worth whatsoever. Non-ET systems have entered the realm of what Nobel Prize–winner Sir Peter Medawar dubs "the limbo of that which is disregarded"[2]— so far off the collective radar of modern musicians that their existence is a non-issue. Even performers who specialize in early music—or historical performance, as it's sometimes called—are to a large extent convinced that ET "took over" around 1800. In fact, as I hope I've demonstrated, ET did take over, but not until around 1917. Before that there was lip service to ET as a standard from about 1850, but that's not what people really wanted to hear, and so that's not what they got. But why, after 1917, was the transition to ET so universal and so complete?

Mark Lindley, one of today's most perceptive and eloquent writers on temperament, attributes it to a number of factors related to the sound of the piano and the styles prevalent at the time:

> Equal temperament in this more exact sense is virtually considered an inherent characteristic of the modern concert piano. Indeed the ideals of sonority in the acoustic design of the modern piano and in all but the more radical forms of modern pianism are as intimately bound to the acoustic qualities of equal temperament as any previous keyboard style ever was to its contemporary style of intonation. The enharmonic facility of Brahms or Fauré, the hovering sonorities of Debussy, the timbral poise of Webern, the slickness of the most urbane jazz chord progressions, all rely implicitly on the hue of equal temperament as much as on the other normal characteristics of the instrument's tone.
>
> Mark Lindley, "Temperaments" in *The New Grove Dictionary of Music and Musicians* (2001)[3]

There is much truth to this. One acoustical characteristic of the modern piano is its "inharmonicity": the tendency of the sounding harmonics of the strings under such enormous tension to rise beyond true harmonic levels, so that tuners have to "stretch" the octaves—making the higher ones higher and the lower ones lower—in order to make them sound in tune across the instrument.* That favors a system where harmonics are not paramount. Furthermore the chromatic ambivalence of twelve-tone music

---

*If the octave harmonics are successively higher than the fundamental, then those notes on the piano will have to be raised to be in tune with the harmonics of the lower note. Using a pitch standard in the middle (A = 440), the effect is a stretching downward of the lower octaves of the piano, and a stretching upward of the higher ones, in order to make the instrument sound in tune across its entire compass.

favors a system in which there is no differentiation among the notes of the scale, with G♯ and A♭ being precisely the same pitch, neither higher as a melodic leading note nor lower as a harmonic one. Also, the nonfunctional harmonic schemes (without leading notes) of Debussy favor whole tones and semitones that are equally spaced. So by 1917 the time was ripe for the regularity of ET. It's also true that the piano of the early twentieth century is essentially the piano of today, and what was good for that piano is good for today's piano because it's the same instrument, even though we use it to play music over a much wider span of time than just 1917 to the present. After a century and a half of experiment and rapid change, the piano all of a sudden became fixed—"petrified," we might say, although the usual view is "perfected"—the design and the action became standardized to a degree never seen before, and increasing mechanization in the manufacturing process made possible its wider distribution:

> By the onset of World War I, as well as being an international instrument, the piano had become universal as well; no longer found mostly in the drawing-rooms of the wealthy, it was now a nearly ubiquitous furnishing and a source of pride and pleasure in even extremely modest homes.
>
> Cyril Erlich and Edwin M. Good, "Pianoforte," in *The New Grove Dictionary of Music and Musicians* (2001)[4]

Such wide distribution also reminds us of the extent to which the piano met the ideals of democracy at this time. What a coincidence that the tuning instructions that finally set the instrument free from even unintentionally unequal tunings were published in the same year as the Russian Revolution—history's ultimate expression of the triumph of "social equality"! Seen in that light, ET becomes almost an expression of political will—a thoroughly democratic musical system in which all notes are created equal and every key is given equal opportunity. The so-called

"American century"—when the American vision of democracy was spread worldwide—thus became the vessel for the safe passage of the most democratic temperament in history, even unto the shores of our own day.

Democracy and capitalism are also reflected in the use of ET in wind instrument design. The late nineteenth century saw a tremendous rise in the number of amateur bands in America, a phenomenon that reached its peak in perhaps the second decade of the twentieth century. Think, for example, of Meredith Willson's *The Music Man*, set in River City, Iowa, in about 1912, and the euphoria surrounding the town's real or imagined band. In Britain the same thing was happening, but the focus was on company bands, like the coal miners' band depicted in the 1996 movie, *Brassed Off*. The need to manufacture so many instruments quickly for this new market forced musical instrument makers to cut corners—to streamline and simplify manufacturing techniques—so that the subtle tuning systems of several nineteenth-century instruments got replaced with basic ET systems.[5] It was so much more convenient and cheaper to make instruments that way. Band music could truly be for the masses, but in a market-driven society, they could afford it only in ET.

Meanwhile there are other philosophical currents to which ET conforms that may help to explain its prevalence and the oblivion of unequal systems. For example, there is an element of positivism in the establishment of ET. Positivism has a long prehistory, but it was articulated in its classic form by Auguste Comte in the middle of the nineteenth century in his *Cours de Philosophie Positive* (Paris, 1830–42). In general terms positivism looks for empirical data to justify knowledge or beliefs. As a result it excludes things that cannot be studied by quantification or that do not fit theories assembled by documented evidence. This means that something so complex and irrational as the division of sounds into a musical scale was bound to prefer the order and apparent simplicity of ET.

ET seemed to have "solved" the temperament problem in a mathematical way and ironed out all the differences between the keys in irregular temperaments. Positivist systems tend to perpetuate themselves by always using the established system as a reference. This phenomenon can be seen in the work of Murray Barbour, who wrote what is generally regarded as the most authoritative history of temperament, originally as a PhD dissertation at Cornell in 1932, and later published in book form. I noted earlier that Barbour once admitted that when he did that work he had never heard anything but ET, and it's clear throughout his discussion that ET is the "center" to which he constantly returns and to which all irregular temperaments are to be compared—unfavorably. For example, he describes a temperament like that of Francesc'Antonio Vallotti—one that is widely and effectively used in performances of eighteenth-century music today (even though I have published my own misgivings about it)—as the "tuning of the out-of-tune piano."* How could unequal tuning systems compete on this basis? Criticizing them from the standpoint of universal utility was self-evident. Nothing was ET but ET. Never mind that, as Poole noted in 1850, all its chords are "equally out of tune."

Owing to the triumph of positivism in science, the early twentieth century saw a decisive victory in the ancient struggle between two philosophies of life: "vitalism" and "mechanism" (or "materialism," as it's sometimes called). The vitalists saw life in the irregularities, the elusive, indefinable aspects of things, while the mechanists saw strength and "progress" in the regularization

*Barbour, *Tuning and Temperament* (East Lansing, Mich., 1951), p. 163. He is actually referring to a temperament recommended at the very end of the eighteenth century by the polymath Thomas Young. It's organized identically to Vallotti's temperament except that it's transposed by a fifth toward the "sharp side." My own work on Vallotti (and Young) was published as the premier article in *Historical Performance Online* (2000), from Early Music America, and may be accessed at www.earlymusic.org/Content/Publications/HistoricalPerformance .htm.

of things. The materialists/mechanists were confident that life could be reduced to a subset of physics, chemistry, and mathematics. If something could be scientifically explained, put into a rational order, then it was closer to a natural truth than something that exhibited what might be called the "messiness of humanity." It is certainly easy to see unequal temperaments as vitalist and ET as fitting a rationalist ideal. What could be more scientifically elegant than dividing the octave into twelve equal parts, while simultaneously tempering each of the twelve fifths by an identical increment? Never mind that, except for the octave, the musical result does not contain a single interval related to the acoustical ratios found in nature. The twentieth century belonged to the mechanists, and their temperament was ET.*

Another philosophical theory that seems to contribute to the hegemony of ET in the early twentieth century is that of "monism," which is clearly expressed in the following statement by Harold Joachim, T. S. Eliot's tutor at Oxford (and coincidentally the nephew of the celebrated violinist):

> That the truth itself is one, and whole, and complete, and that all thinking and all experience move within its recognition and subject to its manifest authority. This I have never doubted.
>
> Harold H. Joachim, *The Nature of Truth* (1906)[6]

In any scientific study, there is an inherent desire for a "theory of everything," for a way to explain a complex system or systems by the simplest means possible, and to embrace that theory as "the whole truth." After the myriad attempts throughout history to divide the octave, to temper some or all fifths by greater or

---

*One related link between the mechanists and sound occurred in 1916, when sonar was first used in the sinking of a submarine. If sound could form part of the scientific apparatus for underwater detection, and be deployed successfully for military purposes, then it had really "arrived," from a mechanistic point of view.

lesser amounts, to balance euphony with utility, it must have been a relief in a way, to have a truly equal temperament at last. But I'm here to say that the monotheistic religion of ET is a false one, that the "limbo of the disregarded" for unequal temperaments is over, that in this post-modern world we are ready to recognize that ET is not the best musical solution nor the most appropriate historical solution for much of the music being performed today, and that we are ready for, indeed, we embrace the reality of what music can be—to borrow pragmatist William James's famous phrase—in its "booming, buzzing confusion."[7]

CHAPTER TEN

Where Do We Go from Here?

No true harmonic ideas are based on equal temperament.
DONALD FRANCIS TOVEY, "Harmony,"
in *Encyclopædia Britannica* (1929)[1]

ANYONE WHO GREW UP in the older, more flexible system and was a fine and sensitive musician (like Donald Francis Tovey, for example) understood what was lost by the universal adoption of ET. It is not a system that favors harmonic performance, much less harmonic thinking. Anyone born after the beginning of the twentieth century had virtually no awareness of *non*-ET systems, so they were never in a position to judge what was good and what was bad about ET. And armed with the certainty of that oblivion, they could dismiss anything but ET as mere historicism. The chinks in that armor appeared with the rise of the historical performance movement and the gradual insistence that "early music" needed to be in an appropriate historical temperament—although among mainstream professionals it was still possible to see this as "very nice for the classroom," as Itzhak Perlman once said about the historical performance movement in general.[2]

Sir Donald Francis Tovey

Sir Donald Francis Tovey, music scholar, composer, and pianist, was born in Eton on July 17, 1875, and died at Edinburgh on July 10, 1940. Though the son of a master at Eton College, he was educated at home by Sophie Weisse, who prepared him for a career as a concert pianist. Tovey was a precocious musician and had already begun to compose by the age of eight. In June 1894, he became the first Lewis Nettleship scholar at Balliol College, Oxford.

Sir Donald Francis Tovey. (*Tovey Archive, Edinburgh University*)

That same year, he appeared with Joseph Joachim, with whose quartet he continued to perform until 1914. Early in the century, he seemed to be establishing himself as a virtuoso pianist and esteemed composer, with successful performances of his works in London, Berlin, and Vienna.

In July 1914 Tovey was appointed Reid Professor of Music at Edinburgh University, though he never saw himself as part of the fraternity of musicologists, whose company he disliked, and he found the biographical aspects of music history boring. Nonetheless, in 1914–15 he presented a series of historical concerts at the university and, in 1917, founded the Reid Orchestra, thus initiating that organization's long and still vital role in Edinburgh's cultural life. Tovey's extensive series of insightful, witty, and wide-ranging program notes for the Reid were subsequently published in six volumes as *Essays in Musical Analysis* (1935–39), and he wrote several articles for the fourteenth edition of *Encyclopædia Britannica* (1929). He was knighted in 1935.

As a conductor, Tovey brought great insight to the works he directed, but conducting was not really his forte. His combination of intellect, verbal virtuosity, musical understanding, and artistry made him extraordinary, however. Perhaps no more surprising tribute can be found than the following by a famous musician with whom Tovey collaborated on several occasions:

The fact is I regard Tovey as one of the greatest musicians of all time.

Pablo Casals, Joys and Sorrows (1970)[3]

Even now, however, it is common to hear people say, echoing Murray Barbour, that Bach's music sounds hideous in anything other than ET. They could even ascribe to Bach the ultimate justification for ET with his famous *Well-Tempered Clavier*, whose forty-eight preludes and fugues explore each of the twelve major and minor keys. Whatever temperament you use for, say, Telemann as a choice for historical performance, Bach could always be an exception and validate the triumph of ET. Those days ended for good in early 2005 when keyboard scholar and performer Bradley Lehman deciphered and published Bach's encoding of the temperament he intended for his famous collection.[4] There is no question that Lehman convincingly solved Bach's puzzle, and the bad news for defenders of ET in Bach is that Bach's temperament is not ET. It is unique but nonetheless one of the family of circulating temperaments—with similar kinds of tempered intervals to those of Bach's contemporary Johann Georg Neidhardt, for example—usable in all keys but shaded to favor slightly some keys over others. In fact, the "sample" irregular temperament given back in figure 7 is Bach's own "well temperament" as deciphered by Lehman. This was Bach's ideal for keyboard music, not ET. So, in spite of his highly chromatic writing in all keys, ET defenders can no longer claim Bach as their secret champion, as the man who was such a great musician that he anticipated and justified the ultimate victory of ET in the modern era.

What does this mean for us? I think it means that we need to look again at the tuning systems used by the great composers and performers throughout history—for anyone, in fact, whose music we are performing today. The reason for doing this is not mere historicism; it's because it represents the choice that musicians of those times made themselves in an effort to present their music the way it sounded best to them.

If you are a keyboard player, this means balancing the repertoire you play and the instrument you play with various choices of temperament in which to fix their scales. Some instruments, of course, are more easily tuned than others. If it takes a month to retune an entire organ, that's not something that's going to be done several times a year. Yet, if you are a pianist and what you *most* prefer to play is Mozart or Beethoven, then it may be worth exploring some non-ET possibilities of temperament in which to have your instrument tuned—even if it's a modern Steinway grand. As a sample of how that might sound, there are two CDs by pianist Enid Katahn that present exactly that repertoire on exactly that instrument in various historical temperaments: *Beethoven in the Temperaments* and *Six Degrees of Tonality*.[5] And even if you decide one day to play the Schubert G♭ major Impromptu, would it be so bad to hear it in the temperament that Bach or Mozart felt was fine for use in any key? It wouldn't sound like ET, but maybe it wasn't meant to.

The focus of this book, however, has not been on the various keyboard temperaments, but on what non-keyboard performers should do or can do. String players, wind players, and singers all have some degree of flexibility as to where they place the notes of the scale. Their great advantage, as noted again and again throughout history, is that they are not obliged to put the notes—especially the accidentals—always in the same place, but can choose a placement that fits the harmonic context of the moment. Yet, because these musicians must sometimes perform with keyboard instruments, it makes sense for their systems to be somewhat compatible.

That's why I think it is so striking that Joachim's open strings are so close to those same pitches in the Victorian "ET" documented by Ellis. Does it surprise you that Bach's temperament has fifths that are narrow by that same amount for the open strings of the violin family? And Mozart. Though we have no "Rosetta stone" (as Lehman calls his Bach evidence) for his temperament, yet we can still figure out what Mozart's preferred tuning was like. In analyzing Mozart's table for Thomas Attwood, John Hind Chesnut says the following:

Roughly speaking, these average pitches adhere rather closely to
1/6 comma meantone temperament in the chain of fifths from *c* to
e, and then gradually diverge. . . . This argues against the hypothesis that the temperament in question is equal temperament. . . .
It would appear from this that the two tuning systems being compared in Attwood's annotated interval table are extended regular
meantone temperament for the non-keyboard instruments and
some form of irregular temperament for keyboard instruments.

John Hind Chesnut, "Mozart's Teaching of Intonation" (1977)[6]

Bach agrees. Mozart agrees. The finest piano tuners of the late
nineteenth century agree. One of the greatest violin virtuosos of
the nineteenth century agrees. Who are we to argue with this
unanimity? And these are not mere theorists—mere musical non-
entities. If the keyboard instruments with which one occasionally
plays are set in temperaments that use sixth-comma narrowing of
all of the fifths involved in the open strings of the violin family,
then it makes sense to me that this is where modern players
should start (whether playing with accompaniment or not): by
narrowing their open strings basically twice as much from an
acoustically pure fifth as they normally would if tuning ET. I
know this will be uncomfortable news for a lot of people. String
players *like* to have pure fifths between their strings. It's a com-
fort thing, like silky sand between the toes on a secluded tropical
beach. But experienced string players know that they just can't
afford to tune the open strings pure: that C–E third is just not tolerable that way.*

---

*As with most things, Quantz had a comment on the tuning of open strings:
"Tuning the four fifths wide on the violin causes a considerable difference with
the harpsichord . . . it is a mistake made only by those who consider music as a
mere trade from which they derive no real satisfaction, not by thoughtful and
experienced artists who love music and play in order to please refined ears."
(See Quantz, *Versuch einer Answeisung die Flöte traversiere zu spielen*, chap.
16/7.)

Interestingly even some professional early music players are resistant to this. Even though they rarely play open strings together, even though they may be playing with a keyboard or lute tuned in sixth-comma meantone, and even though they are committed to the kinds of thirds found in sixth-comma meantone, they still don't want to give up their pure fifths. I've had such players tell me they tune pure fifths regardless of the accompanying instrument, but when I measure their open strings in recorded performances on the frequency counter, they are as narrow as the keyboard's fifths. Just like the nineteenth-century tuners who thought they were tuning ET, these string players may think they are tuning pure fifths, but they're not. Besides, earlier violin technique uses more open strings in the course of playing, so those notes need to match the notes of the keyboard.

All I am suggesting is for string players to narrow the open strings a little more than they narrow them for ET. Then, aim to play the major thirds fairly narrow and the minor thirds a little wide. One of the best ways to accomplish this while playing a melodic line is to raise the flatted notes slightly (!) and lower the sharped notes slightly (!). I know that seems counterintuitive, but it will result in a flexible system like the one described by theorists for non-keyboard instruments in the eighteenth century, where A♭ is a little higher than G♯, for example. That's the goal, so that especially the thirds—so neglected as consonances in ET—will move a little more toward their acoustically pure ratios: not all the way—in fact, about half way between ET and pure—but still better. The next "tip" is to play the whole tones a little smaller than in ET and to differentiate the semitones by a comma, making the diatonic semitones larger and the chromatic semitones smaller. For example, a major or minor scale will have only the larger, diatonic semitones (a.k.a. minor seconds), but chromatic semitones—those with the same note name, like C–C♯ or D♭–D—will use the smaller variety of half step.

Once these things have been accomplished, it should be possible to adjust the fifths occasionally by widening them slightly toward purity whenever a chord is held long enough to allow it and the musical situation would be enhanced by doing so. Thus, instead of adjusting the thirds toward purity within an ET model, I suggest adjusting the fifths toward purity within a flexible sixth-comma model. Even though he did not have this in mind, I believe this amounts to the same kind of practical compromise, the same kind of variance from ET, advocated by Arnold Steinhardt of the Guarneri Quartet when he talked about paying attention to the vertical aspects of the texture. The melodic practices I have just been describing result in harmonies that move toward Just intonation, and are closer to extended-sixth-comma meantone than they are to ET. In reality it's not essential, or even possible for that matter, to meet the exact cents figures for these intervals, any more than "expressive intonation" demands or expects an exact deviation from ET. Any movement in the direction indicated will make the harmonies better. In fact, in contradistinction to "expressive intonation," if this system needs a name it could perhaps be called "harmonic intonation."

And while I have spent a lot of time referring to aspects of string playing, singers obviously have complete flexibility to place the notes wherever they want, and are not even constrained by the fixed pitches of open strings. Many people believe that singers should use Just intonation—with pure fifths as well as pure thirds throughout—but, as I said earlier, I'm not convinced that this works for much music after 1700, and I don't think it serves tonal music (that is, any music using functional harmony) as well as the extended-sixth-comma system does. Remember, a singer—Pier Francesco Tosi—was an early advocate of the 55-division, which is essentially the same as extended-sixth-comma meantone.

Wind players should be able to make most of these pitch

adjustments as well. Clearly, the trombone is completely flexible. Trumpet players constantly adjust their valve tuning slides as they play, so although they will have to learn separate positions for flat and sharp notes around the same pitch level, it should be entirely possible. With other instruments, like flute and oboe, for example, it may be more difficult, but players are adept at shading the pitch one way or another (by fingering, breath, or embouchure) and this practice will simply require them to do that same thing, though more often than they are used to in ET. Is this possible? Yes. Is it worth it? I suppose that's for players to decide, once they hear the sound of the music with the notes shaded toward their "proper" positions and away from the compromise of ET. My guess is that the music will sound so good in "harmonic intonation" that the players will find a way to make it happen, even in larger ensembles, in which there will need to be some kind of consensus on the extent of the shading.

This brings us back to the piece of music that gave me the idea for this book. Have I answered the question of why Christoph von Dohnányi couldn't get that Bb-major chord near the beginning of Beethoven's Ninth Symphony to sound right? I hope so. It's because, first of all, the F in the D minor chord needs to be a little higher than in ET in order to be better in tune as a minor third above D. By better in tune, I mean somewhat closer to its acoustically pure position than it would be in ET. Next, the Bb also needs to be a little higher than in ET in order to make a slightly better major third with the D (as well as a good fifth with the now raised F). My guess is that the Bb chord never sounded right to Maestro von Dohnányi and the Cleveland Orchestra because, in such a stark harmonic situation, the wide, jangling major third of Bb–D in ET was acoustically unpalatable. It may be that modern musicians have become inured to the wide major third of ET as a general rule, but in that musical situation, and listening as critically as an imminent Carnegie Hall performance demanded, it didn't sound right anymore. It didn't sound right because, like all ET major thirds, it was so far from acoustical purity.

But what about the "expressive intonation" of Casals? Actually, the recording of Sarasate (who was more that thirty years older) and the analysis of George Bernard Shaw together suggest that Casals was following an already-established Spanish tradition.* As long as the music is for a soloist and the harmonic element is secondary, the higher leading notes of expressive intonation may sound right and be musically gratifying to many people, especially for music closer to our own time. Even Gregorian chant, the "original" unaccompanied melody with no harmony to complicate matters, sounds expressive when its "leading notes" are raised.† And without a chordal accompaniment, where's the harm? When a keyboard or other instruments (or voices) accompany, or where the solo music itself is harmonically oriented, then I think performers need to pay more attention to the vertical aspects of what they are doing. At the very least, it should be acceptable for them *not* to use expressive intonation.

Casals's apologist, David Blum, incredulously describes an

---

*Although, ironically, Casals reportedly liked the intonation of neither Joachim *nor* Sarasate.

†More than forty years ago, acousticians Paul Boomsliter and Warren Creel published two studies suggesting that people preferred Pythagorean thirds *in the absence of vertical constraints*. In other words, wide major thirds and high leading notes seem "natural" as part of a melodic system, regardless of a subject's previous musical background and training. That may be, but what I have been trying to demonstrate here is that most music making is not devoid of harmony and therefore ought to take into account the vertical element. There are acoustical reasons for doing so as well as historical ones. For Boomsliter and Creel's work, see "The Long Pattern Hypothesis in Harmony and Hearing," in *Journal of Music Theory* 5, no. 2 (1961): 2–30, and "Extended Reference: An Unrecognized Dynamic in Melody," in *Journal of Music Theory* 7, no. 2 (1963): 2–22.

occasion in 1960 when a cellist "not without talent" did not initially appreciate the master's "expressive" approach:

> Casals considered it essential that expressive intonation be taught to string players from the beginning of their studies. He took endless trouble in retraining the aural sense and habitual finger placements of students who, since childhood, had unquestioningly applied piano intonation to their stringed instruments. "The effects of any neglect of this kind at the beginning of studies . . . can affect a player through the whole of his career, however gifted he may be." I once met the living proof of this statement in a cellist who was attending Casals' Berkeley classes—a performer not without talent but who had early on been brainwashed by equal temperament. Hearing Casals for the first time, she exclaimed, "It is *soooooo* beautiful—but why does he play out of tune?"
>
> David Blum, *Casals and the Art of Interpretation* (1977)[7]

She might just as well have said, "The Emperor has no clothes." That Casals's approach was the only acceptable one was self-evident to his followers, but this uninitiated player heard the high leading notes for what they really are from an acoustical standpoint: out of tune. I wish I knew what happened to that woman after she spoke so honestly and got held up to ridicule by David Blum. Did she become a convert, or did she continue to follow her own sense of what good tuning was, whether inculcated by ET or born of an innate sense of harmonic tuning?

I said at the outset that I had two basic goals: to show that in some respects ET doesn't sound as good as some of the alternatives, and to show that before the standardization of ET became so overwhelming, musicians knew about ET and in many cases chose not to use it. My success in those areas—and I hope you agree that I have demonstrated them successfully—should cause modern musicians to reconsider their exclusive use of ET for every kind of music. I also believe that the one variance from ET accepted by most modern musicians—"expressive intonation"—

Pablo Casals

Pablo Casals, the cellist, con- ductor, pianist, and composer, was born in Vendrell, Catalo- nia, on December 29, 1876, and died in Puerto Rico on October 22, 1973. Son of musi- cal parents, he first played piano, organ, and violin before deciding on cello at age eleven. His experiments in technique produced an origi- nal style and a previously unheard-of virtuosity on the instrument. His discovery of the Bach Unaccompanied Suites fostered his serious approach to music and became a lifetime fascination. In 1893 the Spanish Queen Regent, Maria Christina, sponsored him in studies at the Madrid

Pablo Casals in 1962.
(Copyright Lebrecht Music & Arts)

works only for soloistic situations and not for a lot of the playing that musicians do, including chamber music and orchestral music. It's time, in fact, to explore "harmonic intonation" as a way of enhancing the vertical quality of any music that uses tonal har- mony, no matter when it was composed or for what performance medium.*

---

*Even within a basic ET approach, performers may find that understanding harmonic intonation helps them solve tuning puzzles that, in the past, have defied solution.

Conservatory, and in 1895 at Brussels. After a short stint as second cello at the Folies-Marigny music hall in Paris, he returned to teach in Barcelona in 1896.

Never flashy, he sought truth and beauty and used his remarkable powers with uncompromising simplicity and concentration. He is solely responsible for the emergence of the cello as a premier solo instrument, really for the first time. In 1919 he helped to establish the École Normale de Musique in Paris and, also in that year, the Orquestra Pau Casals, a Barcelona-based group that achieved a very high standard of performance. Always socially conscious, Casals was especially proud of their series of concerts for workers.

Under threat of execution by the Franco regime, Casals moved in 1936 to Prades, a Catalan village on the French side of the Spanish border. In 1945, after realizing that the Allies were not going to move against the oppressive Franco regime, Casals vowed not to play in public again. He broke that silence for the Bach bicentenary of 1950, when many distinguished musicians joined him at Prades. He then began a new series of recordings. Casals later directed festivals at Perpignan and in Puerto Rico, where he finally settled in 1956, afterward venturing out only rarely—often for performances in support of world peace.

I am perfectly aware that what I am suggesting is a radical idea for musicians and that it is likely to be met with reluctance, resistance, and even scorn in some quarters. Some musicians will be convinced by my arguments but may still view unequal tuning as a Pandora's box to be opened carefully or not at all; others will scoff at the long historical pedigree of extended meantone as irrelevant; still others will find both the harmonic and melodic intervals strange and "out of tune." At least that's how it may seem to some the first time they hear it or try it. But my experience has been that an hour or so of experimenting over two or three sessions is all that's necessary to help musicians begin, at least, to appreciate what non-ET tuning has to offer from a musical point of view.* As I'm fond of saying, the fact that musicians from earlier times did something is not *in itself* enough justification for musicians of today to follow suit, even though the testimonials of Bach and Mozart have to count for something. What makes it worth trying is that it makes the music sound better. And remember, I'm not saying that harmonic intonation should replace ET entirely and substitute its own tyranny; only that ET is not necessarily the best temperament for every single musical situation encountered by today's musicians.

Before closing, I feel obliged to say a little about vibrato, since subtle tuning techniques can be completely obscured by the use of a wide vibrato. Actually, as treatises and early recordings reveal, vibrato used to be considered an ornament—to sweeten the sound of longer notes—not an integral and constant part of the sound itself, as is often taught today. In fact, it may be that the universal adoption of ET in the early twentieth century contributed to the widening use of vibrato, as performers sensed that it masked some of the unpleasantness of the thirds.[†] At any rate

---

*Citing the "Serendipity Principle," Bruce Haynes observed when he kindly read a draft of this book, "If Mozart expected it that way, there was probably a good reason (which may not be evident to us until we give it a good try)." And as English lawyer and music historian Roger North wrote ca.1726: "And untill a set of musicall *vertuosi*, well weighed in a resolution, and capable to make the experiment, and of whom none, as thinking themselves wiser, shall put on the contemptuous frowne and seem inwardly to sneer, shall be mett together, with all things fitt for the same designe, there will be no reason to expect the antiquitys of musick should ever be understood." See *Roger North on Music*, ed. John Wilson (London, 1959), pp. 283–84. Harmonic intonation surely demands the same kind of open-minded, open-eared effort.

†Recently musicologist Mark Katz speculated that vibrato was a reaction to the difficulty of getting the early phonograph to register the sound of the violin. See his chapter "Aesthetics Out of Exigency: Violin Vibrato and the Phonograph" in

this is not the place to explain how constant vibrato ruined expression; that would be another book. But performers should be aware that the period in which non-ET tunings were standard was also characterized by the use of vibrato only as an ornament. Regardless of your personal taste in vibrato, however, the kinds of tuning adjustments recommended here should still benefit the harmony, since the ear perceives the *center* of the vibrated pitch as the note itself, and simply moving that center toward a purer harmony will make it better.

One final point related to the nonexclusive use of ET: Although I advocate lower leading notes for harmonic purposes, and Casals, on the contrary, advocates higher leading notes for melodic purposes, there is one thing on which he and I agree absolutely when it comes to advising non-keyboard musicians. As he puts it:

> Do not be afraid to be out of tune with the piano. It is the piano that is out of tune. The piano with its tempered scale is a compromise in intonation. Pablo Casals, quoted in *The Way They Play* (1972)[8]

I couldn't have said it better myself. Now go, and do thou likewise.

Capturing Sound: How Technology has Changed Music (Berkeley, 2004). Violinist David Douglass told me that he thought another factor was the desire for string instruments at that period to play louder and louder, since there is a limit to how much pressure can be placed on a bowed string before it begins to sound harmonics rather than the fundamental pitch. Vibrato breaks up the tendency to sound harmonics and thus allows much greater bow pressure and, consequently, a much greater volume of sound from the string.

The rationale is, that if people who are taught music are taught that one thing is right and another wrong, they will come to believe it. If they are taught the other systems of interest as well as the equal temperament, they would appreciate the excellences of all.

R. H. M. BOSANQUET,
*An Elementary Treatise on Musical
Intervals and Temperament* (1876)[9]

Table of Intervals in Cents

Interval	Example	Ratio	Just	ET	Bach WT	Sixth-Comma	55-Division
Minor Semitone	C–C♯	135:128	92.2	100	94-110	88.6	87.3
Major Semitone	C–D♭	16:15	111.7	100	94-110	108.2	109.1
Minor Tone	C–D	10:9	182.4	200	196-204	196.7	196.4
Major Tone	C–D	9:8	203.9	200	196-204	196.7	196.4
Diminished 3rd	C♯–E♭	256:225	223.5	200	196-204	216.3	218.2
Augmented 2nd	C–D♯	75:64	274.6	300	294-306	285.3	283.6
Minor 3rd	C–E♭	6:5	315.6	300	294-306	304.9	305.4
Major 3rd	C–E	5:4	386.3	400	392-406	393.5	392.7
Diminished 4th	C–F♭	32:25	427.4	400	392-406	413.4	414.6
Augmented 3rd	C–E♯	125:96	478.5	500	496-502	482.1	480.0
"Perfect" 4th	C–F	4:3	498.04	500	496-502	501.6	501.8
Augmented 4th	C–F♯	45:32	590.2	600	594-608	590.2	589.1
Diminished 5th	C–G♭	64:45	609.8	600	594-608	609.8	610.9
"Perfect" 5th	C–G	3:2	701.96	700	698-704	698.4	698.2
Augmented 5th	C–G♯	405:256	794.1	800	794-808	787.0	785.4
Minor 6th	C–A♭	8:5	813.7	800	794-808	806.5	807.3
Major 6th	C–A	5:3	884.4	900	894-906	895.1	894.6
Augmented 6th	C–A♯	225:128	976.5	1000	996-1004	983.7	981.8
Minor 7th (lesser)	C–B♭	16:9	996.1	1000	996-1004	1003.3	1003.6
Minor 7th (greater)	C–B♭	9:5	1017.6	1000	996-1004	1003.3	1003.6
Major 7th	C–B	15:8	1088.3	1100	1094-1106	1091.9	1090.9
Diminished 8ve	C–C♭	256:135	1107.8	1100	1094-1106	1111.4	1112.7
Augmented 7th	C-B♯	2025:1024	1180.4	1200	1200	1180.4	1178.2
8ve	C–C	2:1	1200.0	1200	1200	1200.0	1200.0

Notes: As with the two Ds and the two B♭s, there are other possible Just ratios for some of these intervals: for example, 25:24 for a smaller minor semitone (70.7c), 25:16 for an augmented fifth (772.6c), and 125:64 for an augmented seventh (1158.9c). In this table I have given intervals that come closer to our usual scale.

Endnotes

PRELUDE

1. E. Michael Frederick, "Some Thoughts on Equal Temperament Tuning" (unpublished essay).
2. Stuart Isacoff, *Temperament: The Idea That Solved Music's Greatest Riddle* (New York, 2001).
3. Barbour's statement about Bach appears in his *Tuning and Temperament* (East Lansing, Mich., 1951), p. 196. His comment about not having heard anything besides equal temperament occurs in a 1948 letter to A. R. McClure, cited by Mark Lindley in "Temperaments," § 8, in *The New Grove Dictionary of Music and Musicians* (New York and London, 2001).

CHAPTER 1: SHOULDN'T LEADING NOTES LEAD?

1. William Gardiner, *The Music of Nature* (London, 1832; American ed. Boston, 1837), p. 433.
2. Arthur H. Benade, *Fundamentals of Musical Acoustics* (New York, 1976), p. 275.

CHAPTER 2: HOW TEMPERAMENT STARTED

1. Sir Percy Buck, *Proceedings of the Musical Association* 66 (1940), p. 51.
2. Robert Smith, *Harmonics, or the Philosophy of Musical Sounds*, 2nd ed. (London, 1759), p. 166.
3. Johann Georg Neidhardt, *Gäntzlich erschöpfte, mathematische Abteilungen des diatonisch-chromatischen, temperirten Canonis Monochordi* (Königsberg, 1732); trans. Mark Lindley, "Temperaments," §5, in *The New Grove Dictionary of Music and Musicians* (New York and London, 2001).
4. Hermann von Helmholtz, *Die Lehre von den Tonempfindungen als physiologische Grundlage für die Theorie der Musik* (Brunswick, 1863), p. 519; trans. Alexander J. Ellis, *On the Sensations of Tone* (London, 1875), p. 500. For the 1885 edition, Ellis changed "pianoforte" to "clavier" (pp. 321–22).
5. *Versuch über die wahre Art das Clavier zu Spielen* (Berlin, 1753), p. 10; trans.

William J. Mitchell, *Essay on the True Art of Playing Keyboard Instruments* (New York, 1949), p. 37.

CHAPTER 3: NON-KEYBOARD TUNING

1. Bruce Haynes, "Beyond Temperament: Non-Keyboard Intonation in the 17th and 18th Centuries," *Early Music* 19 (1991), p. 357.
2. Pier Francesco Tosi, *Opinioni de' Cantori* (Bologna, 1723), pp. 12–13; trans. after Johann Ernst Galliard, *Observations on the Florid Song* (London, 1743), pp. 19–21.
3. Leopold Mozart, *Versuch einer gründlichen Violinschule* (Augsburg, 1756), ch. 3, sec. 6; trans. after Editha Knocker, *Treatise on the Fundamental Principles of Violin Playing* (London, 1948), p. 70n.
4. This is a quote from Mayor Shin in Meredith Willson's *The Music Man* (1962).
5. Johann Joachim Quantz, *Versuch einer Anweisung die Flöte traversiere zu spielen* (Berlin, 1752), ch. 17, sec. 6.20, p. 232; trans. after Edward R. Reilly, *On Playing the Flute*, 2nd ed. (London, 1985), p. 260.
6. Ibid, ch. 3, sec. 8; trans. after Edward R. Reilly, *On Playing the Flute*, 2nd ed. (London, 1985), p. 46.

CHAPTER 4: "HOW LONG, O LORD, HOW LONG?"

1. Donald Francis Tovey, *Beethoven* (ca. 1936; pub. London, 1944), p. 41.
2. *The Art of Quartet Playing: The Guarneri Quartet in Conversation with David Blum* (New York, 1986), p. 28.
3. David Boyden, "Prelleur, Geminiani, and Just Intonation," *Journal of the American Musicological Society* 4 (1951): 202–19; a response refuting that notion appeared the following year in J. Murray Barbour, "Violin Intonation in the 18th Century," *JAMS* 5 (1952): 224–34. For a discussion of an actual, if briefly noted, approach to Just intonation for strings in the eighteenth century, see Neal Zaslaw, "The Complete Orchestral Musician," *Early Music* 7 (1979): 46–57.
4. See in particular my "Just Intonation in Renaissance Theory and Practice," *Music Theory Online* 12 (2006): http://mto.societymusictheory.org/issues/mto.06.12.3/toc.12.3.html.
5. *The Art of Quartet Playing: The Guarneri Quartet in Conversation with David Blum* (New York, 1986), p. 30.
6. Ibid., p. 31.

CHAPTER 5: A BRIDGE TO THE NINETEENTH CENTURY

1. Luigi Picchianti, *Principi Generali e Ragionati della Musica Teorico-Pratica* (Florence, 1834), p. 101.
2. Daniel Gottlob Türk, *Klavierschule* (Leipzig and Halle, 1789), p. 43; trans. after Raymond H. Haggh, *School of Clavier Playing* (Lincoln, Neb., 1982), p. 426.

3. Ibid., p. 45; trans. p. 53.

4. Michel Woldemar, *Grande Méthode* (Paris, 1798–99/1802–3), p. 4.

5. Quoted in Horst Walter, "Haydn's Klaviere," *Haydn-Studien* 2 (1970): 270–71. See also Carl Ferdinand Pohl, *Mozart und Haydn in London*, (Vienna, 1867), p. 194; Joseph Haydn, *Gesammelte Briefe und Aufzeichnungen*, ed. Dénes Bartha (Kassel, 1965), no. 178, p. 283.

6. Anton Felix Schindler, *Biographie von Ludwig van Beethoven* (Münster, 1860); trans. after Constance S. Jolly, ed. D. W. MacArdle, *Beethoven as I Knew Him* (Chapel Hill, N.C., 1966), p. 367.

7. The most extensive discussion of key characteristics, including the role of unequal temperaments, is in Rita Steblin, *A History of Key Characteristics in the Eighteenth and Early Nineteenth Centuries*, 2nd ed. (Rochester, N.Y., 2002).

8. Pietro Lichtenthal, *Dizionario e Bibliografia della Musica* (Milan, 1826), trans. after John Hind Chesnut, "Mozart's Teaching of Intonation," *Journal of the American Musicological Society* 30 (1977): 255.

9. H. W. Poole, "An Essay on Perfect Musical Intonation in the Organ," *American Journal of Science and Arts*, 2nd ser., ix (1850): 199–200.

10. Hermann von Helmholtz, *Die Lehre den Tonempfindungen als physiologische Grundlage für die Theorie der Musik* (Brunswick, 1863), p. 503; trans. Alexander J. Ellis, *On the Sensations of Tone* (London, 1875), p. 482/(1885), p. 310.

11. Philippe Marc Antoine Geslin, *Cours Analytiques de Musique, ou Méthode Développée du Méloplaste* (Paris, 1825), pp. 228–29.

12. See Pierre Galin, *Exposition d'une Nouvelle Méthode pour l'Enseignement de Musique* (Paris, 1818), pp. 80n, 107n, 161n. Galin's division is the same as that recommended by the Dutch theorist Christiaan Huygens in the seventeenth century, although Galin seems to have been unaware of the precedent.

13. Charles Édouard Joseph Delezenne, "Sur les Valeurs Numériques des Notes de la Gamme," in *Recueil des Travaux de la Société de l'Agriculture et des Arts de Lille* (1826–27): 47.

14. Ibid., p. 55.

CHAPTER 6: REALLY BETTER OR SIMPLY EASIER?

1. H. W. Poole, "An Essay on Perfect Musical Intonation in the Organ," *American Journal of Science and Arts*, 2nd ser., ix (1850): 71.

2. Louis Spohr, *Violinschule* (Vienna, 1832), p. 3; trans. Robin Stowell, *Violin Technique and Performance Practice in the Late Eighteenth and Early Nineteenth Centuries* (Cambridge, 1985), p. 253.

3. Ibid.

4. Ibid.

5. François-Antoine Habeneck, *Méthode Théorique et Pratique de Violon* (Paris, ca. 1835), p. 7n.

6. Ibid., p. 78; trans. Robin Stowell, *Violin Technique and Performance Practice*

in the Late Eighteenth and Early Nineteenth Centuries (Cambridge, 1985), pp. 255–56.

7. Bernhard Romberg, *A Complete Theoretical and Practical School for the Violoncello* (ca. 1839); trans. (Boston, n.d.), pp. 22, 120.
8. Ibid., p. 121.
9. Ibid., p. 122.

CHAPTER 7: SOME ARE MORE EQUAL THAN OTHERS

1. H. W. Poole, "An Essay on Perfect Musical Intonation in the Organ," *American Journal of Science and Arts,* 2nd ser., ix (1850): 204.
2. Hermann von Helmholtz, *Die Lehre den Tonempfindungen als physiologische Grundlage für die Theorie der Musik* (Brunswick, 1863); Alexander J. Ellis, "Additions by the Translator," in *On the Sensations of Tone* (London, 1885), p. 548.
3. Alexander J. Ellis, "Additions by the Translator," in *On the Sensations of Tone* (London, 1885), pp. 548–49.
4. Ibid., p. 549.
5. Owen Jorgensen, *Tuning* (East Lansing, Mich., 1991), p. 3.
6. Alexander J. Ellis, "On the Temperament of Musical Instruments with Fixed Tones," *Proceedings of the Royal Society of London* 13 (1864): 419.
7. Alexander J. Ellis, "Additions by the Translator," in *On the Sensations of Tone* (London, 1885), p. 485.
8. Owen Jorgensen, *Tuning* (East Lansing, Mich., 1991), p. 538. He refers to the result as a "Victorian" temperament.

CHAPTER 8: THE "JOACHIM MODE"

1. Albert Lavignac, *Music and Musicians*, trans. William Marchant (1899; first pub. 1895), pp. 53–54.
2. Paul David, "Joachim, Joseph," in George Grove, ed., *A Dictionary of Music and Musicians* (1890), vol. 2, pp. 34–35.
3. Hermann von Helmholtz, *Die Lehre den Tonempfindungen als physiologische Grundlage für die Theorie der Musik* (Brunswick, 1863), p. 525; trans. Alexander J. Ellis, *On the Sensations of Tone* (London, 1885), p. 325.
4. 1875 edition, pp. 790–91; 1885 edition, pp. 486–87.
5. George Bernard Shaw, *London Music in 1888–89 as Heard by Corno di Bassetto (Later Known as Bernard Shaw) with Some Further Autobiographical Particulars* (New York, 1937), pp. 331–32.
6. George Bernard Shaw, *Music in London, 1890–1894*, vol. 2. (London, 1932), pp. 276–77.
7. Donald Francis Tovey, "The Joachim Quartet," in *Times Literary Supplement,* May 16, 1902, pp. 141–42.
8. Donald Francis Tovey, "Joseph Joachim," in *Times Literary Supplement*, Aug. 23, 1907, pp. 257–58.

9. Alphonse Blondel, "Le Piano et sa Facture," in *Encyclopédie de la Musique et Dictionnaire du Conservatoire* (Paris, 1913), p. 2071.

CHAPTER 9: "THE LIMBO OF THAT WHICH IS DISREGARDED"

1. James Lecky, "Temperament," in *A Dictionary of Music and Musicians* (Grove 1) (London, 1890), vol. 4, p. 73.
2. P. B. Medawar and J. S. Medawar, *Aristotle to Zoos: A Philosophical Dictionary of Biology* (Cambridge, Mass., 1983), p. 277.
3. Mark Lindley, "Temperaments," §8, in *The New Grove Dictionary of Music and Musicians* (New York and London, 2001).
4. Cyril Erlich and Edwin M. Good, "Pianoforte," I, §8, in *The New Grove Dictionary of Music and Musicians* (New York and London, 2001).
5. That process as it pertains to the flute, for example, is described in Ardal Powell, *The Flute* (New Haven, 2002), pp. 199–203.
6. Harold H. Joachim, *The Nature of Truth* (Oxford, 1906), p. 178.
7. This much-quoted phrase is from James's *Principles of Psychology*, vol. 1 (New York, 1890), p. 488. He actually said "blooming," however.

CHAPTER 10: WHERE DO WE GO FROM HERE?

1. Donald Francis Tovey, "Harmony," in *Encyclopædia Britannica*, 14th ed. (1929).
2. Itzhak Perlman (interview with Jeremy Siepmann), "All Play Is Work," *BBC Music Magazine* 3 (May 1995): 23.
3. Pablo Casals, *Joys and Sorrows: Reflections, by Pablo Casals as told to Albert E. Kahn* (New York, 1970), p. 215.
4. Bradley Lehman, "Bach's Extraordinary Temperament: Our Rosetta Stone," *Early Music* 33 (2005): 3–23, 211–31. A selection of responses, some laudatory, some quibbling, some opposed, appears on pp. 545–48 of the same volume.
5. Gasparo GSCD-332 (1997) and Gasparo GSCD-344 (2000), respectively.
6. John Hind Chesnut, "Mozart's Teaching of Intonation," *Journal of the American Musicological Society* 30 (1977): 268–70.
7. David Blum, *Casals and the Art of Interpretation* (New York, 1977), p. 108.
8. Pablo Casals, quoted in Samuel and Sada Applebaum, *The Way They Play*, vol. 1 (Neptune City, N. J., 1972), p. 272.
9. R. H. M. Bosanquet, *An Elementary Treatise on Musical Intervals and Temperament* (London, 1876), p. 40.

Select Bibliography

Attwood, Thomas, and W. A. Mozart. *Thomas Attwoods Theorie- und Komposi-tionsstudien bei Mozart.* Ed. E. Hertzmann, C. B. Oldman, D. Heartz, and A. Mann. Wolfgang Amadeus Mozart: *Neue Ausgabe sämtlicher Werke*, X:30/i. Kassel: Bärenreiter, 1965.

Barbieri, Patrizio. "Violin Intonation: A Historical Survey." *Early Music* 19 (1991): 69–88.

Barbour, J. Murray. *Tuning and Temperament: A Historical Survey.* East Lansing: Michigan State College Press, 1951.

———. "Violin Intonation in the 18th Century." *Journal of the American Musicological Society* 5 (1952): 224–34.

Benade, Arthur H. *Fundamentals of Musical Acoustics.* New York: Oxford University Press, 1976; reprint, New York: Dover Publications, 1990.

Blackwood, Easley. *The Structure of Recognizable Diatonic Tunings.* Princeton, N. J.: Princeton University Press, 1985.

Blondel, Alphonse. "Le Piano et sa Facture." *Encyclopédie de la Musique et Dictionnaire du Conservatoire*, vol. 3, part 2, pp. 2061–72. Paris: C. Delagrave, 1913.

Blum, David. *The Art of Quartet Playing: The Guarneri Quartet in Conversation with David Blum.* New York: Alfred A. Knopf, 1986.

———. *Casals and the Art of Interpretation*, New York: Holmes and Meier, 1977.

Boomsliter, Paul and Warren Creel. "The Long Pattern Hypothesis in Harmony and Hearing." *Journal of Music Theory* 5 no. 2, (1961): 2–30.

———. "Extended Reference: An Unrecognized Dynamic in Melody." *Journal of Music Theory* 7 no. 2 (1963): 2–22.

Bosanquet, R. H. M. *An Elementary Treatise on Musical Intervals and Temperament.* London: Macmillan, 1876.

Boyden, David. "Prelleur, Geminiani, and Just Intonation," *Journal of the American Musicological Society* 4 (1951): 202–19.

Burgess, Geoffrey, and Bruce Haynes. *The Oboe*. New Haven, Conn.: Yale University Press, 2004.

Campagnoli, Bartolomeo. *Nuovo Metodo della Mecanica Progressiva* (1797?); parallel Italian/French edition, *Nouvelle Méthode de la Mécanique Progressive du Jeu de Violon*. Florence: Ricordi, 1815?; facsimile, *Méthodes et Traités* 13, série 4, vol. 3. Courlay, France: J. M. Fuzeau, 2002.

Chesnut, John Hind. "Mozart's Teaching of Intonation." *Journal of the American Musicological Society* 30 (1977): 254–71.

Comte, Auguste. *Cours de Philosophie Positive*. Paris: Bachelier, 1830–42.

Delezenne, Charles Édouard Joseph. "Sur les Valeurs Numériques des Notes de la Gamme." *Recueil des Travaux de la Société de l'Agriculture et des Arts de Lille* (1826–27): 1–71.

Duffin, Ross W. "Why I Hate Vallotti (or is it Young?)." *Historical Performance Online* 1 (2000), www.earlymusic.org/Content/Publications/HistoricalPerformance.htm, from Early Music America.

———. "Baroque Ensemble Tuning in Extended 1/6 Syntonic Comma Meantone." *Digital Case* (2006): http://hdl.handle.net/2186/ksl:rwdbar00.

———. "Just Intonation in Renaissance Theory and Practice." *Music Theory Online* 12 (2006): http://mto.societymusictheory.org/issues/mto.06.12.3/toc.12.3.html.

Ellis, Alexander J. "On the Temperament of Musical Instruments with Fixed Tones," *Proceedings of the Royal Society of London* 13 (1863–64): 404–22.

———. "Additions by the Translator." In Hermann von Helmholtz, *On the Sensations of Tone*. Appendix 20, pp. 430–556. London: Longmans, Green, 1885; reprint, New York: Dover Publications, 1954.

———. "On the Musical Scales of Various Nations." *Journal of the Society of Arts* 33 (1884–85): 485–527.

Frederick, E. Michael. "Some Thoughts on Equal Temperament Tuning" (unpublished essay).

Galin, Pierre. *Exposition d'une Nouvelle Méthode pour l'Enseignement de Musique*. Paris, 1818; partial trans. Bernarr Rainbow, *Rationale for a New Way of Teaching Music*. Kilkenny, Ireland: Boethius Press, ca.1983.

Gardiner, William. *The Music of Nature*. London: Longman, 1832; Boston: Ditson, 1837.

Geslin, Philippe Marc Antoine. *Cours Analytiques de Musique, ou Méthode Développée du Méloplaste*. Paris: Geslin, 1825.

Habeneck, François-Antoine. *Méthode Théorique et Pratique de Violon*. Paris: Canaux, ca.1835; facsimile, *Méthodes et Traités* 9, série 2, vol. 4. Courlay, France: J. M. Fuzeau, 2001.

Haydn, Josef. *Josef Haydn: String Quartet in F, 1799, Hoboken III: 82: Reprint of the Original Manuscript*. Ed. László Somfai. Budapest: Editio Musica; Melville, N.Y.: Belwin Mills, ca. 1980.

Haynes, Bruce. "Beyond Temperament: Non-Keyboard Intonation in the 17th and 18th Centuries." *Early Music* 19 (1991): 357–81.

Helmholtz, Hermann von. *Die Lehre den Tonempfindungen als physiologische Grundlage für die Theorie der Musik* (1863); trans. Alexander J. Ellis, *On the Sensations of Tone*, 3rd ed. 1875; 4th ed. 1885.

Isacoff, Stuart. *Temperament: The Idea that Solved Music's Greatest Riddle*. New York: Alfred A. Knopf, 2001; rpt. with an "Afterword" as *Temperament: How Music Became a Battleground for the Great Minds of Western Civilization*. New York: Vintage Books, 2003.

Joachim, Harold H. *The Nature of Truth*. Oxford: Clarendon Press, 1906.

Jorgensen, Owen. *Tuning the Historical Temperaments by Ear: A Manual of Eighty-Nine Methods for Tuning Fifty-One Scales on the Harpsichord, Piano, and Other Keyboard Instruments*. Marquette: Northern Michigan University Press, ca. 1977.

———. *Tuning: Containing the Perfection of Eighteenth-Century Temperament, the Lost Art of Nineteenth-Century Temperament, and the Science of Equal Temperament, Complete with Instructions for Aural and Electronic Tuning*. East Lansing: Michigan State University Press, 1991.

Katz, Mark. *Capturing Sound: How Technology has Changed Music*. Berkeley: University of California Press, 2004.

Lecky, James. "Temperament." *A Dictionary of Music and Musicians* (Grove 1) vol. 4. London: Macmillan, 1890, pp. 70–81.

Leedy, Douglas. "A Personal View of Meantone Temperament." *The Courant* 5 (1983): 3–19.

Lehman, Bradley. "Bach's Extraordinary Temperament: Our Rosetta Stone." *Early Music* 33 (2005): 3–23, 211–31.

Lindley, Mark. "A Suggested Improvement for the Fisk Organ at Stanford." *Performance Practice Review* 1 (1988): 107–32.

———. "Interval" and "Temperaments." *The New Grove Dictionary of Music and Musicians*. New York and London: Macmillan, 2001.

———. "Stimmung und Temperatur." In *Geschichte des Musiktheorie 6: Hören, Messen und Rechnen in der Frühen Neuzeit*. Darmstadt: Wissenschaftliche Buchgesellschaft, 1987.

Lloyd, Llewelyn. S., and Hugh Boyle. *Intervals, Scales, and Temperaments.* New York: St. Martin's Press, 1963.

Marpurg, Friedrich Wilhelm. *Neue Methode allerley Arten von Temperaturen dem Claviere aufs Bequemste.* Berlin: Haude & Spener, 1755; facsimile of 2nd edition (1765), Hildesheim: G. Olms, 1970.

Medawar, Peter B., and J. S. Medawar. *Aristotle to Zoos: A Philosophical Dictionary of Biology.* Cambridge, Mass: Harvard University Press, 1983.

Mozart, Leopold. *Versuch einer gründlichen Violinschule.* Augsburg: J. J. Lotter, 1756; facsimile, Kassel: Bärenreiter, 1995; trans. Editha Knocker, *Treatise on the Fundamental Principles of Violin Playing.* London and New York: Oxford University Press, 1948.

Neidhardt, Johann Georg. *Gäntzlich erschöpfte, mathematische Abteilungen des diatonisch-chromatischen, temperirten Canonis Monochordi.* Königsberg: C. G. Eckarts, 1732.

Picchianti, Luigi. *Principi Generali e Ragionati della Musica Teorico-Pratica.* Florence: Tipografia della Speranza, 1834.

Poole, H. W. "An Essay on Perfect Musical Intonation in the Organ," *American Journal of Science and Arts*, 2nd ser., ix (1850): 68–83, 199–216.

Powell, Ardal. *The Flute.* New Haven: Yale University Press, 2002.

Prelleur, Peter. *The Modern Musick-Master, or The Universal Musician.* London, 1730/1; facsimile, *Documenta Musicologica* 1:27. Kassel: Bärenreiter, 1965.

Quantz, Johann Joachim. *Versuch einer Anweisung die Flöte traversiere zu spielen* (1752); facsimile, Kassel: Bärenreiter, 2000; trans. Edward R. Reilly, *On Playing the Flute.* 2nd ed. London: Faber and Faber, 1985; reprint Boston: Northeastern University Press, 2001.

Romberg, Bernhard. *A Complete Theoretical and Practical School for the Violoncello* (ca. 1839); trans. Boston: Ditson, 1855.

Smith, Robert. *Harmonics, or the Philosophy of Musical Sounds.* Cambridge: J. Bentham, 1749; 2nd ed., London: T. and J. Merrill, 1759.

Spohr, Louis. *Violinschule.* Vienna: T. Haslinger, 1832; facsimile, Munich: Katzbichler, 2000; trans. John Bishop, *Louis Spohr's Celebrated Violin School.* London: R. Cocks, 1843; trans. *Spohr's Grand Violin School.* Boston: Ditson, 1852.

Steblin, Rita. *A History of Key Characteristics in the Eighteenth and Early Nineteenth Centuries.* Ann Arbor: UMI Research Press, 1983; 2nd ed. Rochester, N.Y.: University of Rochester Press, 2002.

Telemann, Georg Philip. *Neues musicalisches System* (1742–43); published in Lorenz C. Mizler: *Neu eröffnete musikalische Bibliothek* 3–4. Leipzig, 1752; facsimile, Hilversum: E. Knuf, 1966.

Select Bibliography

Tosi, Pier Francesco. *Opinioni de' Cantori.* Bologna, 1723; facsimile, *Monuments of Music and Music Literature in Facsimile* 2:133. New York: Broude Brothers, 1968; trans. Johann Ernst Galliard, *Observations on the Florid Song.* London, 1743; trans. Johann Friedrich Agricola, *Anleitung zur Singkunst.* Berlin, 1757.

Tovey, Donald Francis. *Beethoven.* London: Oxford University Press, 1944 (written ca. 1936).

———. "Harmony," *Encyclopædia Britannica,* 14th ed. London, New York, 1929.

Türk, Daniel Gottlob. *Klavierschule.* Leipzig and Halle, 1789; facsimile, *Documenta Musicologica* 1:23. Kassel: Bärenreiter, 1962; trans. Raymond H. Haggh, *School of Clavier Playing.* Lincoln: University of Nebraska Press, 1982.

———. *Anleitung zu Temperaturberechnungen.* Halle, 1808; facsimile, Halle: Händel-Haus, 1999.

Vallotti, P. Francesc'Antonio. *Della Scienza Teorica, e Pratica della Moderna Musica libro primo.* Partial ed. Padua: Giovanni Manfrè, 1779; complete ed. *Trattato della Moderna Musica.* Padua: Basilica del Santo, 1950.

White, William Braid. *Modern Piano Tuning and Allied Arts.* New York: E. L. Bill, 1917.

Woldemar, Michel. *Grande Méthode.* Paris: Cochet, 1798–99/1802–03; facsimile, *Méthodes et Traités* 9, série 2, vol. 1. Courlay, France: J. M. Fuzeau, 2001.

Young, Thomas. "Of the Temperament of Musical Intervals." *Philosophical Transactions of the Royal Society of London for the Year 1800.* London: Royal Society, 1800.

Zaslaw, Neal. "The Compleat Orchestral Musician." *Early Music* 7 (1979): 46–57.

Sources and Permissions

Bio Images (in alphabetical order)

ATTWOOD: Lithograph frontispiece of Thomas Attwood by F. Waller to *Attwood's Cathedral Music*, edited by the composer's godson, Thomas Attwood Walmisley (London: Ewer, 1850?). Courtesy of Kent State University Library, Department of Special Collections.

BLONDEL: Alphonse Blondel, photo portrait from Alfred Dolge, *Pianos and Their Makers* (Covina, 1911); reprint, New York: Dover Publications, p. 254. Portrait inscribed "À Monsieur Alfred Dolge. Amical Souvenir du Successeur de Sebastian Erard. A. Blondel. Paris 20 Avril 1911."

BRAID WHITE: William Braid White photographing noise in Chicago (September 30, 1930). Original caption: "On the theory that noise is nothing more than a waste of mechanical energy, Dr. William Braid White, director of acoustic research for the American Steel and Wire Company, a subsidiary of the United States Steel Corporation [*sic*] is gathering data for the Noise Commission of Chicago with this new machine which photographs the noise by changing it into a beam of light and then recording it on a sensitive film." Copyright Underwood & Underwood/Corbis.

CAMPAGNOLI: Engraving from Bartolomeo Campagnoli's *Nuovo Metodo della Mecanica Progressiva* (1797?); earliest surviving edition (Florence: Ricordi, 1815?), plate 1, following p. 40. Reprinted from the facsimile edition, *Méthodes et Traités* 13, série 4, vol. 3 (Courlay, France: 2002), with the kind permission of Éditions J. M. Fuzeau.

CASALS: Pablo Casals playing in Carnegie Hall (1962). Copyright Lebrecht Music & Arts.

DELEZENNE: Portrait drawing of Charles Édouard Joseph Delezenne, courtesy of the Collection École Polytechnique, Lille.

ELLIS: Alexander J. Ellis, robed to receive his LittD at Cambridge on June 10, 1890. Portrait by Colin Lunn, Cambridge, reproduced from Jaap Kunst, *Musi-*

cologica (Amsterdam, 1950). p. 8; 3rd, enlarged edition published as *Ethnomusicology* (The Hague: Martinus Nijhoff, 1969), p. 217. Labeled in autograph handwriting, "This is Alexander Ellis as I remember him. G. Bernard Shaw. Ayot Saint Lawrence [Hertfordshire] 28 November 1949." Reprinted with permission of the Indisch Wetenschappelijk Instituut, The Hague.

GALIN: Frontispiece engraving by Lacoue of Pierre Galin teaching, from his *Exposition d'une Nouvelle Méthode pour l'Enseignement de Musique*. Paris, 1818.

HABENECK: François-Antoine Habeneck, portrait drawing by L. Massard, Paris. Copyright Lebrecht Music & Arts.

HELMHOLTZ: Hermann von Helmholtz, portrait photograph ca. 1885. Photo by Hulton Archive/Getty Images.

HIPKINS: Alfred J. Hipkins, portrait painting (1898) by his daughter Edith J. Hipkins (d. ca. 1940). Courtesy of the National Portrait Gallery, London.

JOACHIM: Joseph Joachim, portrait photograph by Johanna Eilert (1903). Copyright Lebrecht Music & Arts.

L. MOZART: Portrait engraving of Leopold Mozart from his *Versuch einer gründlichen Violinschule* (Augsburg, 1756). Reprinted from the facsimile edition (Kassel, 1995) by permission of Bärenreiter Music Corporation.

PACHMANN: Vladimir de Pachmann, from a Baldwin Piano Company advertisement (1925) in the collection of the author.

PRELLEUR: Engraving detail from *The Modern Musick-Master, or the Universal Musician* (London, 1730–31), frontispiece to section 6: The Harpsichord. Reprinted from the facsimile edition, *Documenta Musicologica* 1:27 (Kassel, 1965) by permission of Bärenreiter Music Corporation.

PYTHAGORAS: Detail from Franchino Gafurius's *Theorica Musice* (1492), B6r. Reprinted from the facsimile edition, *Monuments of Music and Music Literature*, in Facsimile 2:21 (New York, 1967), with the kind permission of Broude Brothers.

QUANTZ: Johann Joachim Quantz, engraving by [J. F. W.?] Schleuen. The image originally appeared as the frontispiece to *Allgemeine deutsche Bibliothek* 4 (Berlin and Stettin: Friedrich Nicolai, 1767). Courtesy of the Dayton C. Miller Collection, Music Division, Library of Congress.

SARASATE: Pablo de Sarasate, portrait photograph (ca. 1900). Copyright Lebrecht Music & Arts.

SMITH: Robert Smith, portrait (1730) by John Vanderbank (1694–1739). Reproduced by kind permission of the Master and Fellows of Trinity College, Cambridge.

SPOHR: Louis Spohr, self-portrait. Copyright Lebrecht Music & Arts.

Tosi: Engraving detail from *The Modern Musick-Master, or The Universal Musician* (London: 1730–31), frontispiece to section 1: An Introduction to Singing. Reprinted from the facsimile edition, *Documenta Musicologica* 1:27 (Kassel, 1965), by permission of Bärenreiter Music Corporation.

Tovey: Portrait photo from the Tovey Archive, Edinburgh University. Used by permission.

Türk: Portrait engraving from the Bärenreiter Archive. Reprinted from the frontispiece to the facsimile edition of Türk's *Klavierschule* (1789), *Documenta Musicologica* 1:23 (Kassel, 1962), by permission of Bärenreiter Music Corporation.

Woldemar: Michel Woldemar's chart of note values from his *Méthode d'Alto* (Paris: Cousineau, 1800–1805), p. 1. Engraved by Van-ixem. Reprinted from the facsimile edition, *Méthodes et Traités* 5, série 1 (Courlay, France: 2000), with the kind permission of Éditions J. M. Fuzeau.

Figures

Figure 8: Fingerboard diagram. Peter Prelleur, *The Modern Musick-Master, or The Universal Musician* (London, 1730–31), section 5: "The Art of Playing on the Violin," between pp. 4 and 5. From the facsimile edition, *Documenta Musicologica* 1:27 (Kassel, 1965), by permission of Bärenreiter Music Corporation.

Figure 11: British Library Additional MS 58437: The Attwood Manuscript. Exercises in theory and composition by Thomas Attwood (b. 1765, d. 1838) with autograph corrections by W. A. Mozart. Detail of fol. 1/4. Courtesy of the British Library.

Figure 12: Fingerboard diagram. Bartolomeo Campagnoli, *Nuovo Metodo della Mecanica Progressiva* (1797?); earliest surviving edition (Florence: Ricordi, 1815?), p. 129. Reprinted from the facsimile edition, *Méthodes et Traités* 13, série 4, vol. 3 (Courlay, France: 2002), with the kind permission of Éditions J. M. Fuzeau.

Figure 13: Chromatic scale detail. Michel Woldemar, *Grande Méthode* (Paris: Cochet, 1798–99/1802–3), p. 3. Reprinted from the facsimile edition, *Méthodes et Traités* 9, série 2, vol. 1 (Courlay, France: 2000), with the kind permission of Éditions J. M. Fuzeau.

Figure 14: Haydn autograph manuscript of his String Quartet in F (1799) Hoboken III: 82, from National Széchényi Library, Budapest. Reprinted from the facsimile edition by Belwin Mills Publishing Corporation (ca. 1980) with the kind permission of Alfred Publishing.

FIGURE 15: Cello part fragment from the first edition (1802) of Haydn's String Quartet in F (Hoboken III: 82). Reprinted from the facsimile edition by Belwin Mills Publishing Corporation (ca. 1980) with the kind permission of Alfred Publishing.

Cartoons

All cartoons were drawn by Philip Neuman expressly for this book and are printed with his kind permission.

Index

Note: Numbers in *italics* indicate illustrations.

semitones in, 40, 42, 52

sociological and philosophical connections, 140–44

twelve-tone music and, 17

vibrato and, 158–59

Erard piano firm, 108–9, 136

Erlich, Cyril, 140

Essays in Musical Analysis (Tovey), 147

Expériences et Observations . . . (Delezenne), 91

Exposition d'une Nouvelle Méthode pour l'Enseignement de la Musique (Galin), 87–90, 92

"expressive intonation," 19–20, 52, 69, 71–75, 78–79, 133–35, 137, 154–56

extended-fifth-comma meantone temperament, 55, 92–93

extended meantone fifth "spiral," 56

extended-quarter-comma meantone temperament, 55, 92

extended-sixth-comma meantone temperament, 53, 55, 56, 70–75, 82, 87, 90, 92, 130n, 132, 133, 150, 152, 157, 159

extended-third-comma meantone temperament, 55

"false consonances," 42

Ferrand, Albert, 123

fifth-comma meantone temperament, 35n, 36, 39
extended, 55, 92–93

fifths
cents in, 115, 163
circle of fifths, 23, 25
early temperament schemes, 31–35, 149
in equal temperament, 27, 38, 67, 69
major third in relation to, 34
pure, 23, 25, 150
in quarter-comma meantone temperament, 33–35
ratio, 23, 25, 27, 32
in sixth-comma meantone temperament, 53n
string instruments and, 130–33, 149, 150–52

flute playing, 57–59, 61–63, 153

fourths
cents in, 163
in equal temperament, 27
ratio, 27, 32

Frederick, E. Michael, 15, 108–9, 118

Frederick the Great, king of Prussia, 63

frequencies, 20, 21, 32–33

fundamental note, 21, 22

Gafurius, Franchino, 24

Galeazzi, Francesco, 44, 72n, 78

Galin, Pierre, 87–90, 89, 92, 102

Galin-Paris-Chevé Method, 87, 90

Gardiner, William, 18

Gasparini, Francesco, 63

George III, King of England, 66

George IV, King of England, 67

Geslin, Philippe Marc Antoine, 88–90, 102

Good, Edwin M., 140

"good temperaments," 37. *See also* "well temperaments"

Grand Traité d'Instrumentation et d'Orchestration Modernes (Berlioz), 103n

Grande Méthode (Woldemar), 79

Gray & Davison firm, 108

Great Exhibition of 1851 (London), 106–7

Greene (organ builder), 108

Gregorian chant, 154

Grenser, Carl Augustin, 61

Grove, George, 116

Guarneri Quartet, 69–70, 74, 152

Habeneck, François-Antoine, 96–97, 99–103, *100*

"harmonic intonation," 152, 153, 156–59

harmonic series, 20–23, 32–33

Harmonics, or the Philosophy of Musical Sounds (Smith), 42–43

harmony
equal temperament and, 18
"expressive intonation" and, 19–20, 69, 129

harpsichords, 116, 150n

Harrison, John, 43

Hasse, Johann Adolf, 59, 63

Hawkins, John, 43

Haydn, Franz Joseph
String Quartet in F Major, Op. 77, no. 2, 79–82, 84, 87
Telio-chordon and, 84–85
tunings as understood by, 80–82, 84–85, 102

Haynes, Bruce, 46, 111, 158n

Heiligenstadt Testament (Beethoven), 85

Helmholtz, Hermann von, *106*
biography of, 106–7
on C. P. E. Bach, 44
Ellis's translation of, 105, 110, 114–15
equal temperament viewed by, 86
experiment with Joachim, 122–23

Herbert, George, 107

hertz (Hz), 20, 32–33

Hickson, G., 114

Hill, T. (organ builder), 107, 114

in Just intonation, 70
in meantone temperaments,
39, 71–72
pure, 27, 29, 31–35, 48, 69,
72, 92, 115
Pythagorean, 29, 71, 130–31,
154n
ratio, 27, 32
string instruments and, 47–48,
151
in well temperament, 40
Marpurg, Friedrich Wilhelm,
44, 109
tenth temperament, 109n
materialism, 142–43
Mattheson, Johann, 72n
Maxwell, James Clerk, 43
meantone temperaments
19-division system, 55, 92n
31-division system, 55, 92
43-division system, 55, 92
50-division system, 42–43, 92n
53-division system, 55,
135–36n
55-division system, 53, 55, 56,
66, 71, 92, 133, 135,
137, 152
defined, 34, 39
extended systems, 39
fifth-comma, 35n, 36, 39, 55,
92–93
keyboard instruments and, 39,
45n, 104–5, 108
ninth-comma, 104

quarter-comma, 32–35, 39,
54, 55, 92
semitones in, 52, 74–75
sixth-comma, 35n, 36, 39, 53,
54, 55, 56, 70–75, 87,
90, 92, 132, 133, 150,
151, 152, 157, 159
third-comma, 55
mechanism, 142–43
Medawar, Peter, 138
melodic intonation, 19–20, 69,
103n, 133–35, 154–57
Mendel, Arthur, 111
Mendelssohn, Felix
Attwood and, 67
Joachim and, 119, 120–21, 128
Pachmann's performances of,
117
Méthode d'Alto (Woldemar),
83
*Méthode Théorique et Pratique
de Violon* (Habeneck),
96–97, 99–103
Microtonal Études (Black-
wood), 55
Middle Ages, tuning in, 23, 31
minor semitones
cents in, 163
defined, 52, 71
in extended meantone tem-
perament, 39
Galin's proposal for, 87–90, 92
Mozart's understanding of,
65–67

semitones. *See also* major semitones; minor semitones
cents in, 115, 163
in Debussy's music, 140
in equal temperament, 40, 42, 52
Galin's views on, 87, 90
in meantone temperaments, 39, 74–75
L. Mozart's views on, 56–57
Quantz's views on, 61–62
ratios for, 92, 92n
Spohr's views on, 95–97
Tosi's views on, 48, 51, 57, 71, 92
Türk's views on, 76
in well temperament, 39
seventh chords, 36
Seymour (piano tuner), 105
Shaw, George Bernard
    Joachim viewed by, 123–24, 126–27, 129
    Pygmalion, 110
    Sarasate viewed by, 126, 133, 154
Silbermann, Gottfried, 72n
singing
    author's recommendations on, 152
    tuning and, 48, 51, 53, 56, 63, 70, 78, 149
Six Rêves d'un Violon Seul (Woldemar), 83
sixth-comma meantone temperament, 35n, 36, 39, 54, 56, 151
    cents in, 163
    extended, 53, 55, 56, 70–75, 82, 87, 90, 92, 130n, 132, 133, 150, 157, 159
    flexible model for strings, 152
Smith, Robert, 40, 42–43, 43, 92n
Sobel, Dava, 43
"social equality," 140–41
Société des Concerts du Conservatoire, 101
sonar, 143n
Sorabji, Kaikhosru, 117
sound waves, 20
Spain, temperaments in, 108, 133, 154
split keyboards, 39, 45n, 51, 52, 84–85
Spohr, Louis, 81, 94–97, 96, 102
Steinhardt, Arnold, 69–70, 73, 152
string playing
    author's recommendations on, 151–52
    "expressive intonation" and, 19–20
    French school, 120
    Habeneck's views on, 99, 102–3
    Joachim's practices, 119–33
    open strings tuning, 130–33, 149, 150–52